THE CELEBRATION
OF THE GOSPEL

THE CELEBRATION
OF THE GOSPEL

A STUDY IN CHRISTIAN WORSHIP

h. grady hardin
joseph d. quillian, jr.
james f. white

ABINGDON PRESS — NASHVILLE • NEW YORK

THE CELEBRATION OF THE GOSPEL

ISBN 0-687-04799-4

Library of Congress Catalog Card Number: 64-15760

MANUFACTURED BY THE PARTHENON PRESS AT
NASHVILLE, TENNESSEE, UNITED STATES OF AMERICA

TO OUR COLLEAGUES IN WORSHIP AND STUDY

laity
ministers
students
faculty

preface

There is more interest in Christian worship now than at any previous time in this century. Most of the attention is directed to the meaning rather than to the means of worship. The focus is evangelical rather than aesthetic. The desire is to understand worship in the context of the whole gospel, and to relate it to the whole of Christian living. The practical concern is to worship God in a way that is in keeping with his revelation of himself in Jesus Christ. No one any longer speaks of "enriching our worship services," as if services of Christian worship were optional human ceremonies designed primarily to induce certain psychological effects in people.

The principal influences upon the renewal of worship are our need for help beyond ourselves in this age of sustained crisis; the serious biblical, theological, and historical studies which have resulted in a more adequate understanding of the gospel as well as new familiarity with worship in the New Testament church and the early church; and the movement toward closer relationship among the different churches which necessarily has called for our becoming aware of mutual and essential beliefs and practices with regard to worship. The emphases in the renewal of worship are the wholeness of the gospel in our worship; biblical preaching and the essential unity of sermon and sacrament; the participation of the laity; and the utility of the physical settings and the procedures for helping the people to worship. Whatever impressive beauty there may be in the church building or in the ceremony, such beauty has its place only as it enables people to worship God in Christ.

It should be noted that preaching occupies a central place in Christian worship. Consequently, we would hold that a sermon normally should be preached in every service of corporate worship. Especially should a sermon of appropriate length be preached in the service of Holy Communion. Let us steadfastly avoid the setting of sacrament over against sermon. The emphasis on preaching and sacrament together is a major inheritance within our Wesleyan tradition, and may indeed be the principal contribution that Methodists have to make to the present conversations among the churches concerning Christian worship.

There are numerous excellent studies of Christian worship, both general and specialized. With this in mind, we are providing an extensive structured bibliography. There seems, however, to be the need for a brief basic study which treats Christian worship under a unifying motif, and which intentionally is in accord with the doctrinal standards of Methodism. This is the purpose of *The Celebration of the Gospel*.

The making of this book has been even more of a collaboration than the triple authorship would denote. Most of what is written here has been tried in seminary classrooms, in pastors' schools, in leadership-training classes, in conversations with faculty colleagues, and in discussions in local churches. The students, ministers, teachers, and laymen with whom we have been in conversation have had a considerable part in shaping what we have set down. The procedure that we have followed is that of talking through the general conception and the basic structure of the book, and then parceling out among us the principal responsibilities for the various chapters. All three of us have edited the rough draft of each chapter, and then have gone over it when put into final form.

We do not suppose that we have turned out a piece of work that needs no more changing. Rather, we hope that this modest study may enter in lively fashion into the ongoing discussions concerning worship, and so may prompt insights that go beyond our own.

H. Grady Hardin

Joseph D. Quillian, Jr.

James F. White

contents

11

Chapter 1

THE CELEBRATION OF GOD'S VICTORY

Christian worship always is celebration. This is so because a victory is the basis of Christian worship. It is the victory of Almighty God through Jesus Christ. It is God's victory over our death and for our life; it is the triumph of his purpose to redeem his whole creation to willing responsiveness to him. It is a victory that was won in principle by the death and resurrection of Jesus Christ, and now is to be realized in full. Because it is victory, the whole telling forth (announcing, proclaiming) of what God has done, will do, and is doing through Jesus Christ is called the gospel—"good news." It is "good news" that calls for thankful rejoicing in a different way from any other good news, for God's victory through Jesus Christ is the single source of meaning and hope for our lives. Christian worship, then, however solemn or exuberant, however simple or elaborate, has its meaning in the victorious love of God. Therefore, a Christian funeral is as surely celebration as is a Christian marriage service; and a quiet family prayer on any evening, as surely as a festival Communion on Easter Day. Whatever is done in Christian worship is done as a participation in God's victory through Jesus Christ.

Christian worship is the doing of God. God the Father offers to us his saving love through God the Son, and God the Holy Spirit opens our hearts to the Father's love and enables us to respond to him in joyful acceptance and obedience, which is worship. We cannot, in fact, worship as Christians except as we are enabled by the Holy Spirit. For the one thing that chiefly is affirmed by us in Christian worship, whether in sermon, scripture lesson, creed, hymn, or act of dedication, is that Jesus Christ is Lord. And as Paul tells us, "No one can say 'Jesus is Lord' except by the Holy Spirit." (I Cor. 12:3*b*.) So Christian worship is not simply a response to the gospel, but is a participation in it.

The work of the Holy Spirit further identifies Christian worship as distinct from anything that is done by men of themselves. Article VIII of the Methodist Articles of Religion states:

The condition of man after the fall of Adam is such that he cannot turn and prepare himself, by his own natural strength and works, to faith, and calling upon God; wherefore we have no power to do good works, pleasant and acceptable to God, without the grace of God by Christ preventing us [that is, going ahead of us and enabling us], that we may have a good will, and working with us, when we have that good will.

The grace of God is the power of God effecting his purpose in the hearts of men. This is the work of the Holy Spirit. This means that God is at work on both sides of Christian life and worship—on his side, offering the gift of life in Christ to us; and on our side, accepting the gift through faith. For faith itself is the gift of God the Holy Spirit.

14

In the words of Luther's *Preface to Romans:*

Faith is something that God effects in us. It changes us, and we are reborn from God. What a living, creative, active, powerful thing faith is! It cannot do other than good at all times. It never waits to ask whether there is some good work to do; rather, before the question is raised, it has done the deed, and keeps on doing it. Faith is a living and unshakeable confidence, a belief in the grace of God so assured that a man would die a thousand deaths for its sake. This kind of confidence in God's grace makes us joyful, high-spirited, and eager in our relations with God and with all mankind. It is impossible, indeed, to separate works from faith, just as it is impossible to separate heat and light from fire.[1]

There is, then, no such thing as "God on the one hand and a man on the other" in the work of redemption, as if God does something on his own and then we do something on our own. It is not so simple as "God's action and man's response." This is something that we really already know in our hearts in Christian experience. This is why "Just as I am, without one plea, but that thy blood was shed for me" speaks to the depths of so many Christians. We know that it is God in Christ who saves us, and not we ourselves. Though we emphasize the importance of decision, and rightly so, we never hear a Christian say, "I congratulate myself for having been so wise to have made the right decision." Rather, a Christian says, "Thanks be to God who gives us the victory!"

Christian worship serves God's purpose to bring his children into a community of faith, at one with him and with one another. Consequently, Christian worship is doubly celebration with God. In

[1] From *Reformation Writings of Martin Luther,* tr. with introduction and notes from the definitive Weimer edition by Bertram Lee Woolf (London: Lutterworth Press, 1956), II, 288-89.

worship we praise God and give thanks to him for who he is and for what he does; and in worship he continues to reveal who he is, and continues to do his work in us for which we praise and give thanks to him. Also, Christian worship is celebration with other Christians of all times and places. All Christians are members together of the community of living faith that is the church. In worship, we continue to find together new dimensions of the meaning and way of life as members of the community of faith. Christian worship is celebration that relates us to God and to one another, renewing us in the meaning and power of God's victory in Jesus Christ.

The Central Content of Christian Worship

The victory of God in Christ brings the gift of new life to us. Through Jesus Christ, God reveals himself to be the sovereign Creator and Governor of all things and of all men, who acts with love and power to redeem his whole creation from death to eternal life. "And this is eternal life, that they know thee the only true God, and Jesus Christ whom thou hast sent." (John 17:3.) To know God in Jesus Christ is to know God as *our God,* that it is he that has made us and not we ourselves, that we are dependent upon him for life, for the meaning of life, and for the power to live it. It is to find ourselves in Christ—to know through him who we ought to be and are not; to become through him who we cannot be by our own efforts—the children of God who are loved into life.

"Life in Christ" is vital trust in God that opens us to him in joyful dependence, that interprets all things in the light of his victorious love, and that enables us to accept and to be accepted by one another.

God forgives us into new life in Christ. When God forgives a person, he affirms him in new being. He effects his very being by forgiveness, drawing him out of the bondage of guilt into the freedom, fullness of life, and joy that he wills for us all. He puts us in a new relationship of trust in him. He cuts us loose from the death of wrong-being and reunites us to himself in the life of new being.

This "forgiveness from death into life" is the heart and force of John Wesley's Aldersgate experience. It is "trust in Christ and Christ alone" and the "assurance that he had taken away my sins, even mine" that caused the strange warming of the heart, and that enabled John Wesley to forgive those who had despitefully used him, to testify openly as to his experience, and to live in peace and victory after "the transport of joy" had passed.

I think it was about five this morning that I opened my Testament on those words, "there are given unto us exceeding great and precious promises, even that ye should be partakers of the divine nature." Just as I went out, I opened it again on those words, "thou art not far from the kingdom of God." In the afternoon I was asked to go to St. Paul's. The anthem was, "Out of the deep I have called unto thee, O Lord. O let thine ears consider well the voice of my complaint. If thou, Lord, wilt be extreme to mark what is done amiss, O Lord, who may abide it? For there is mercy with thee; therefore shalt thou be feared. O Israel, trust in the Lord: For with the Lord there is mercy, and with him is plenteous redemption. And he shall redeem Israel from all his sins." In the evening I went very unwillingly to a society in Aldersgate street, where one was reading Luther's preface to the Epistle to the Romans. About a quarter before nine, while he was describing the change which God works in the heart through faith in Christ, I felt my heart strangely warmed. I felt I did trust in Christ, Christ alone for my salvation; and an assurance was given me that he had taken away my sins, even mine, and saved me from the law of sin and death. I began to pray with all my might for those who had in a more especial manner despitefully used me and persecuted me. I then testified openly to all there what I now first felt in my heart. But it was not long before the enemy suggested, "this cannot be faith; for where is the joy?" Then was I taught that peace and victory over sin are essential to faith in the Captain of our salvation; but that, as to the transport of joy that usually attend the beginning of it, especially in those who have mourned deeply, God sometimes giveth, sometimes withholdeth them, according to the counsels of his own will.[2]

It is worth noting that the surging warmth of heart did not continue, but the certainty of Jesus Christ as Savior and the assurance of forgiveness remained.

So important is forgiveness in Christian worship that we well may look also at a contemporary testimony of life in Christ through forgiveness. This was given by a man who had been a farmer all his working life. He was saying what the gospel meant to him.

For one really to understand the Gospel there are many things that must enter in or take place, or at least that was my experience.

First of all it makes something out of you that you were not. This may be a strange way to say it but that is just exactly what happens. I was once given to hatred, envious of others, and life did not have a purpose. All I could see was hard work, hardships, not much return for the effort put forth. Others seemed to prosper and as I have said I was jealous of them. I could not understand why the hardships. The question was always why did it have to happen to me. There was very little happiness in life but one trial and hardship after another. I guess I thought that I was the only one that had trials and hardships.

Then there came that day while I was working in the field—that glorious experience which I will not try and relate because I do not suppose that I could find the word even to begin to describe it, so will let it remain as the greatest event of my life. It was then that I became that which I was not just a moment ago. Hatred, grudges, jealousy, and all things of this nature seemed to vanish. They were gone and in

[2] Nehemiah Curnock, ed., *The Journal of the Rev. John Wesley* (London: The Epworth Press, 1909), pp. 472-76.

place of them was love, concern for others. Self was lost somewhere. Life instead of being meaningless suddenly semmed to have a purpose. There was a reason for this life that I had never known before. It was at this time that I hung my head in shame and asked God for forgiveness and my asking was not in vain. For God heard and God answered.

It was from this experience that I opened the Bible for the first time in many years to learn of the will of God. The more I read the more I learned of the love of God, of his great love for man and one like me. How he gave his son Jesus Christ that one like me might have life. That one like myself could find a purpose. Had I known these things many years ago it would have saved many a heartache.

This brings us down to the present today, of what the Gospel means to me. Saying it in as few words as possible, a new creature, life with a purpose, life that knows joy and happiness and peace and the hope of eternal life through Jesus Christ.[8]

The tone of celebration is unmistakable in these testimonies of two men. They accord with the testimony of the whole church, for we rightly may say that in our corporate worship the whole church celebrates the forgiveness that is the gift of new life in Christ, which is God's victory in immediate, personal expression.

Hope always results from forgiveness, and is an essential characteristic of those who live in Christ. The basis for our hope is the victory of God. God being God, the ultimate and immediate controlling power of all things, has claimed us into his victory through Jesus Christ, ordains us to hope, and confirms us in it. The substance of hope is the ultimate fulfillment of God's purpose to redeem his whole creation into willing responsiveness to him. Sin, pain, suffering, fearfulness, hatred, perversion, anxiety, sloth, tragedy, idolatry, and death are *actual* and are to be taken seriously,

[8] Curtis Ground, Conference Course of Study School, Perkins School of Theology, 1955.

but they are not *final*. These are the denials—the enemies—of life that God moves victoriously to overcome through Jesus Christ. The hope of the Christian is the knowledge in faith that the full context of our present defeats is the ultimate victory of God. This is a major part of what Paul was talking about in the seventh and eighth chapters of Romans:

So I find it to be a law that when I want to do right, evil lies close at hand. For I delight in the law of God, in my inmost self, but I see in my members another law at war with the law of my mind and making me captive to the law of sin which dwells in my members. Wretched man that I am! Who will deliver me from this body of death? Thanks be to God through Jesus Christ our Lord!—Rom. 7:21-25*a*

I consider that the sufferings of this present time are not worth comparing with the glory that is to be revealed to us. For the creation waits with eager longing for the revealing of the sons of God; for the creation was subjected to futility, not of his own will but by the will of him who subjected it in hope; because the creation itself will be set free from its bondage to decay and obtain the glorious liberty of the children of God. We know that the whole creation has been groaning in travail together until now; and not only the creation, but we ourselves, who have the first fruits of the Spirit, groan inwardly as we wait for adoption as sons, the redemption of our bodies. For in this hope we were saved.   —Rom. 8:18-24*a*

A very meaning of God is "he whose will will at last be done." God is "the victorious One!" This knowledge, this *faith,* enables Christians in the present time to have that strange peace that the world cannot give—a participation now in the ultimate victory of God, even in the midst of the complex difficulties of life as we daily experience it. God is victorious; his love never ceases; his mercies are new every morning; therefore we have hope! (Cf. Lam.

20

3:21-24.) How, then, in Christian worship can we do other than *celebrate* the gospel, for the gospel itself offers the victory of God through Jesus Christ!

The Meaning of Celebration

We now may turn to a detailed look at the meaning of celebration. The old-fashioned Fourth of July festivities will help us.

Parade, memorial service, invocation, patriotic address, national anthem, games, fireworks, and picnic lunch—these were the ingredients. The veterans of the wars in their respective uniforms, the National Guard, the Boy Scouts, the volunteer firemen with their bunting-draped firetruck, and the policemen who could be spared from duty, marched behind the colors and the band through the streets of the small town to the square or park. On the way, they stopped at the war memorial for a brief service in which a wreath was laid at the foot of the monument by the mayor or some honored citizen. On to the park, then, where the flag was raised while all stood at attention and the national anthem was played. After the invocation, there was the patriotic address by governor, senator, congressman, or lawyer from neighboring town. The speaker eloquently paid respects to Columbus, the Pilgrim Fathers, George Washington, Abraham Lincoln, the wars— of Independence, of 1812, Between the States, Mexican, Spanish-American, World Wars I and II. (And now would be added the Korean War.) The history of ideal and deed having been rehearsed, the speaker then exhorted all present to loyalty and service to our country in present and future trials. The patriotic address was followed by the pledge of allegiance, "My Country 'Tis of Thee," and the band's presentation of "Stars and Stripes Forever." These formal actions completed, the crowd broke up for informal but still corporate exultation in potato-sack races, horseshoe pitching, ball games, fireworks, and a picnic lunch, with plenty for everyone.

21

Backing off and taking a look, what went on? What were the essential aspects of this celebration? It seems clear that there were three major ones:

1. **Remembrance.** The remembrance of the past of our country, which remembrance reached forward to the future, thus shedding, from both directions, the light of meaning on the present.
2. **Thanksgiving.** Joyful, solemn, exultant thanksgiving for the guiding care of God and for the faithfulness of our forefathers.
3. **Rededication.** Rededication to faith in God and to the humanitarian principles on which our country was conceived, by which it has endured in the past and hopes to flourish in the future.

Remembrance, thanksgiving, and rededication—these are the essential aspects of celebration.

In Christian worship, we rededicate ourselves to God—we offer to him through Jesus Christ "our selves, our souls and bodies." We accept his offering of new life by the dedicatory offering to him of our lives as they now are, to be done with by God as he would do. This is done always in the offertory, for we offer ourselves along with "the fruits of the labors of our hands." It also may come in the confession, in response to the invitation to Christian discipleship, or in a dedicatory response of the heart at any point in the service.

In Christian worship, we are reidentified as those who live in the hope that is grounded in God's victory in Jesus Christ. We are reconciled into relationship with God and with one another as members of the body of Christ that is the church.

Christian worship is the celebration of God's victory, celebrated with God and with Christians of all time and place.

The Spirit of Christian Worship

We need now to think for a while about the spirit of worship. By spirit we mean the feelings of the worshipers, for worship profoundly involves emotion, engaging us in the central depths of our being. We already have been involved in considering the spirit of worship as we have talked about worship as celebration. The "celebrating spirit" of worship includes several "emotions-with-content," some of which are: the feeling of dependence upon God, trust, openness, thanksgiving, dedication, forgiveness accepted and given, joy, hope, peace community-feeling, and sense of history (awareness of past and future as essential to the meaning of the present).

The spirit of worship upon which we now focus is that of awe—the kind of awe that is an emotion which people feel in the presence of God and nowhere else. This awe is the *definitive* spirit of worship. All emotions or feelings in worship are valid as worship feelings to the extent they accord with awe, for awe is direct, personal relatedness to God who is the object of worship. Consequently, awe is the difference-making element in whether a service of worship primarily is a convocation to talk and sing about God, or whether it primarily is a meeting-time with God.

Awe is the awareness by thought and feeling (the two inseparably together as total, personal responsiveness) that God is God and we are creatures. It is the seeing at once of God's holiness in power and goodness and our creatureliness in weakness and wrongness. It is the vital, overwhelming, experienced awareness that nothing in life has real meaning except our being accepted by God, and that we ourselves cannot cause this acceptance to happen.

One basic and lively discussion of awe is in Rudolf Otto's *The Idea of the Holy*. He holds that God's holiness is made up of power and goodness, and he considers awe chiefly to be the unique responsive feeling to God as mysterious power as distinguishable from God as absolute goodness. Otto coins the word "numinous" from the Latin *numen* (power as spirit, present and felt) to describe the object of this primal feeling of awe. The numinous feeling is not experienced as a subjective emotion, but is so wholly caused by the object of awe (God as mysterious power) as to be experienced as something that has the person rather than something that the person has.

The numinous feeling has several elements. It includes wonder, which is being amazed or "struck dumb"; dread, which is a drawing back in awesome fear (as Moses at the burning bush); fascination, which is being held in attraction by a power that will not let one go; and creature-feeling, which is a unique sensing of dependence upon a power outside oneself.

God is mysterious, unutterable power, present, active, and absolutely controlling. God, who expresses his absolute goodness in his love given through his incarnate Son, crucified and raised up, is inseparably God who is numinous power. God's goodness does not domesticate his power so that contact with God's holiness becomes manageable by us or is less awesome to us. Those who first said, "God is Love," knew God already and continuingly as awesome power who creates, governs, and at last determines the destiny of all things.

The sense of awe in the face of God's goodness and power together is expressed in the old form of "O Come, All Ye Faithful." The first stanza read:

> O come, all ye faithful, triumphantly sing!
> Come, see in the manger the angels' dread King!
> To Bethlehem hasten, with joyful accord;
> O hasten! O hasten! to worship the Lord.

"The angels' *dread* King!" Here is caught up the awe that encompasses us in the presence of mysterious power and inexpressible goodness, for the old meaning of dread is precisely numinous awe.

The last stanza also carries this same sense of awe, for it is not just the gentle Christ-child who is adored, but "true Godhead incarnate, omnipotent Word!"

> To thee, then, O Jesus, this day of thy birth,
> Be glory and honor through heaven and earth;
> True Godhead Incarnate, Omnipotent Word!
> O hasten! O hasten! to worship the Lord.

Or again, who can read the account of the Crucifixion without a sense of numinous awe? The cosmic immensities, as well as the depths of every human soul, are involved in the event at which "there was darkness over the whole land until the ninth hour, while the sun's light failed; and the curtain of the temple was torn in two" (Luke 23:44-45).

Charles Wesley bespeaks our response to the Crucifixion with numinous awe:

> O Love divine, what hast Thou done!
> Th' Incarnate God hath died for me!
> The Father's co-eternal Son
> Bore all my sins upon the tree!
> The Son of God for me hath died:
> My Lord, my Love, is crucified.

God's love is inseparable from his awesome power, and no relationship with God is without this kind of awed wonder. "Thus let us offer to God acceptable worship, with reverence and awe; for our God is a consuming fire." (Heb. 12:28b-29.)

Having said this, we now must go on to say that in normal experience Christians do not know God as power alone. We know him only as he has revealed himself, and he has revealed himself to us in holiness; that is, in the power of his purposeful love. We cannot turn back the clock of awareness so that we really can think as if we didn't know God's revealing of himself through Jesus Christ. We cannot recover the precise outlook of psalmist,

25

prophet, Moses, or Abraham; for what we hear from them inescapably is colored and interpreted by what we know through Jesus Christ. We cannot be simply "Old Testament" in our understanding; much less can we be "primitive man" in our understanding. We *begin* our Christian worship in the church in awareness of the gospel revelation of the character of God. Therefore, the awe that is the spirit of worship in the presence of Almighty God is not separable from the gratitude we feel that God, even God himself, loves us and has given his Son for us.

Motif for Christian Worship

Worship does not have simply content; it also has structure. When structure and content are related in a regular and repeated pattern, we call this a motif. Unless the motif is an adequate one, there is always the danger that the structure will squeeze out some of the essential content. Therefore, when we adopt a motif for Christian worship, it is imperative that we stay steadily clear that our worship is the celebration of the whole gospel of Jesus Christ.

The Isaiah Motif

Many studies of worship in recent years have centered upon the experience of Isaiah as recorded in Isa. 6:1-9 as the definitive motif for worship.

"In the year that King Uzziah died I saw the Lord sitting upon a throne, high and lifted up; and his train filled the temple. Above him stood the seraphim; each had six wings: with two he covered his face, and with two he covered his feet, and with two he flew. And one called to another and said:

> "Holy, holy, holy is the Lord of hosts;
> the whole earth is full of his glory."

26

And the foundations of the thresholds shook at the voice of him who called, and the house was filled with smoke. And I said: "Woe is me! For I am lost; for I am a man of unclean lips, and I dwell in the midst of a people of unclean lips; for my eyes have seen the King, the Lord of hosts!"

Then flew one of the seraphim to me, having in his hand a burning coal which he had taken with tongs from the altar. And he touched my mouth, and said: "Behold, this has touched your lips; your guilt is taken away, and your sin forgiven." And I heard the voice of the Lord saying, "Whom shall I send, and who will go for us?" Then I said, "Here I am! Send me." And he said, "Go. . . ."

This great passage from Isaiah is held to exhibit the essentials of worship, which are identified as adoration, confession, affirmation, and dedication. However, these are all quite human and subjective elements—*man's* adoration, *man's* confession, *man's* affirmation, *man's* dedication. If this is all that we had to go on, worship would be left as a purely human ceremony. Actually, though, the Isaiah passage itself fortunately includes much more—namely, the *initiative of God:* God's awesome presence which calls forth from Isaiah both praise and confession; God's forgiveness of Isaiah's sins; God's call to service; God's commission to service; and God's guiding presence. If the Isaiah passage is to be used as a motif for worship, then surely the determining initiative of God must be given primary emphasis. It is God who saves us, not we ourselves; it is God who is the prime mover in worship, and not we ourselves.

Much indeed may be gained in the Isaiah passage with regard to the understanding of and the inspiration to worship. But it is misleading for us to concentrate restrictedly upon this passage for an understanding of Christian worship, or a motif for it. Christ, Holy Spirit, and church make Christian worship different from any other worship. Christian worship is participation in a continuing historical action of God, and not simply an individualistic and episodic relationship to God as the eternal holy One. All that we know of God as infinite power, awesome presence, creator, ruler judge, and Israel's God is inseparable from our knowledge of him as Redeemer through Jesus Christ. Consequently, our worship of God does not begin simply with his awesome presence as infinite power, wholly other, eternal judge, nor yet as Israel's God. Rather, Christian worship begins with God's love in Jesus Christ, through whom God offers life to us, and makes possible our offering of our lives in him. The love of God revealed in Christ Jesus is the "amazing grace" that is the root of Christian awe, the cause of Christian confession, and the source of Christian joy. The savior-hood and lordship of Jesus Christ, the enabling and empowering work of the Holy Spirit, and the corporateness of the church are part and parcel of God's victory that we celebrate in Christian worship. It is best that they be *within* our basic scriptural reference for worship and not imported into it.

A New Testament Motif

With apologies for the presumption of mixing our weak words with those of the Scriptures, it seems that Christians, speaking in a corporate first person, must say something like this in a paraphrase of Isa. 6:1-9.

In the fullness of time (Gal.), I saw the Lord of Power and Glory, the Creator of the heavens and the earth, come down and take upon himself the form of man and become one with us, to dwell among us, healing, teaching, and preaching the coming kingdom; to die upon the cross for us while we were yet sinners (Rom. 5:8), and to be raised up from the dead by the glory of the Father that we too might walk in newness of life (Rom. 8:4); to ascend into heaven as Lord; and to send the Holy Spirit to be Counselor and Comforter until he shall come again to fulfill his work of redemption.

After this I looked, and behold, a great multitude which no man could number, from every nation, from all tribes and peoples and tongues, standing before the throne and before the Lamb, clothed in white robes, with palm branches in their hands, and crying out with a loud voice, "Salvation belongs to our God who sits upon the throne and to the Lamb!" (Rev. 7:9-10.)

And the Holy Spirit took the veil away and made my heart to say, "Jesus Christ is Lord!" (I Cor. 12:3; also second stanza of Charles Wesley's "Spirit of Faith, Come Down"). And I fell upon my knees and said, "O God, I have sinned against heaven and before thee, and am not worthy to be called thy son (Luke 15:18-19), for I have chosen the death of sin when thou hast offered the life of faith." For now my eyes had seen the Lord Jesus Christ, and in him the love of God!

Then God said to me, "Your sins are forgiven for Jesus' sake!" (I John 2:12.)

And I heard the voice of God saying: "You are a chosen race, a royal priesthood, a holy nation, God's own people, that you may declare the wonderful deeds of him who called you out of darkness into his marvelous light. Once you were no people but now you are God's people; once you had not received mercy but now you have received mercy." (I Pet. 2:9-10.)

And I said, "Lord, how can I declare thy wonderful deeds?" And he said, "If you love me, you will keep my commandments. . . . And the Counselor, the Holy Spirit, whom the Father will send in my name, he will teach you all things, and bring to your remembrance all that I have said to you. . . . And when he comes, he will convince the world of sin and of righteousness and of judgment. . . . I have said this to you, that in me you may have peace. In the world you have tribulation; but be of good cheer, I have overcome the world." (John 14:15, 26; 16:8, 33.)

In Christian worship we indeed adore God, confess our sins to him, affirm our faith in him, and dedicate our lives to him. But all this we do principally in mindfulness of what God is doing toward us—his Word to us through Scripture, sermon, assurance of forgiveness, and benediction. All this we do within the corporate fellowship of faith that is the church, by the enabling of the Holy Spirit, and because our worship is a participation in the whole saving action of God in Jesus Christ. Whatever the motif that we use, surely we can intend no less than the celebration of the whole gospel of Jesus Christ in Christian worship.

The Disciplines of Worship

Christian worship is distinguished from all other kinds of worship by the fact that it is the worship of those who being "united with Christ, form one body, serving individually as limbs and organs to one another" (N.E.B.). In other words, its nature is that it is the corporate worship by the body of Christ. Christian worship, then, is not just any worship. By its corporate nature in Christ, it is sharply distinguished from the worship of religions of the East and also from some types of Western mysticism. The idea of the solitary individual alone with "his" God may appear in some religions, but this concept is not compatible with Christianity, which insists that the worshiper be united to other Christians in his worship whether they are physically present or not.

Christian worship is the worship of God's people. Ultimately their worship depends upon God's action in Christ which has made them a new people. The church is those who are "grateful for receiving a kingdom that cannot be shaken." No matter how far apart they may be in the dimensions of space and time, Christians are at one in what they receive, including the possibility of worship through Jesus Christ. As I John expresses it: "That which we have seen and heard we proclaim also to you, so that you may have fellowship with us; and our fellowship is with the Father and with his Son Jesus Christ." (1:3.) This "common life" in

Christ is reflected in all Christian worship thereby distinguishing it from every other kind of worship.

The sense of corporate action in Christ is a constant characteristic of all Christian worship; however, circumstances and occasions necessitate *two* distinct disciplines by which it is expressed. These are personal devotions and common worship. These types of worship are called "disciplines," for it should be clear that Christian worship is not haphazard or by chance. Discipline applies to worship as much as it does to any other aspect of the Christian life. As Paul advises in I Corinthians, "All things should be done decently and in order." (14:40.)

In Christianity both the discipline of personal devotions and the discipline of common worship are corporate in their nature, though this corporateness is expressed by different means. Neither discipline is superior to the other; they merely complement one another. Each suffers when the other is neglected, for each presupposes the other. Yet they do have some quite different characteristics.

The discipline of personal devotions is characterized, of course, by the fact that the individual is not immediately dependent upon the presence of others. He may be separated in time or space from all other Christians in whose worship he nevertheless is joined. On the other hand, he may be in the midst of those engaged in common worship and be pursuing his private devotions instead. A Roman Catholic saying his rosary during Mass or a Protestant engaging in his own prayers in the midst of an anthem are examples of personal devotions in the midst of common worship.

Personal devotions are distinguished from common worship in that there is no need for verbal communication. As a consequence, personal devotions may occur without words being used. Thus they can easily develop out of a feeling of gratitude, awe, or dependence upon God. The beauties of nature, music, and architecture can contribute to personal devotions.

31

There is a great freedom for emotions in personal devotions. Since these devotions are not communicated to others, the emotional latitude is almost unlimited. The heights of ecstatic rapture or the depths of self-accusing contrition are included in the range of personal devotions. Naturally the emotional tone varies from individual to individual, since this form of worship so directly reflects the situation of each person. It should be remembered, however, that personal devotions in Christianity are a corporate act of the body of Christ rather than simply the actions of isolated individuals. The body of Christ transcends the limitations of space and time and includes the worship of all its members, however physically remote from one another they may be.

The experience of Christendom has been that personal devotions, though free, do require a definite discipline in order to fulfill themselves. Even when directed to the devotional life of the individual, there do seem to be some constants in the discipline of personal devotions. The matter of time is important here. Without being legalistic, a set pattern of daily devotions seems helpful. Though the Spirit may blow where it will, it also seems to favor habits. Through the centuries, the Bible has been a prime source for personal devotions among both Protestants and Catholics. This book of the Christian community plays as important a part in personal devotions as it does in common worship. Other books, many of them based on the Bible, also play an important part in the discipline of personal devotions. Quite frequently the Roman Catholic priest, reading his breviary daily, is exposed to the Bible more than is his Protestant counterpart. Meditation, too, involves a discipline which at first glance seems deceptively simple, but turns out to be a difficult exercise. Unfortunately the necessity of discipline in personal devotions is never grasped by many sincere persons who realize, often with a sense of guilt, that something is amiss in their devotional life.

The discipline of common worship is different in several ways from that of personal devotions. One would be quite mistaken to consider common worship simply the sum total of various personal devotions. No term describes common worship better than the word "liturgy." The Greek term *leitourgia* refers to the performance of a public task imposed upon all who were citizens at Athens. It was simply fulfilling the responsibility of a citizen, doing the expected service of anyone who was a part of the city. Basically the term derives from two Greek words—the word *leitos,* meaning people, and the term *ergon,* meaning work. In the Christian church the same concept remained, only the liturgy was the work of a new people, the people of God. To be a Christian implied doing this *leitourgia,* and indeed the term "church" was probably originally applied to the liturgical assembly. It is wrong to think of liturgy as something fancy and complicated. It may be the simplest sort of service in the plainest possible meetinghouse, consisting of preaching, praying, reading the Bible, and singing. Even so, it is liturgy, for liturgy is the performing of the work of the people of God, in short, common worship.

But in order for common worship to be possible, a very definite discipline is necessary. This involves three means, which we may call structure, words, and actions.

It is impossible to play baseball without knowing that a team has nine members on the field at one time, that a batter gets three strikes and only three strikes, and that a run may be scored only by touching all four bases. Likewise, common worship demands an agreement as to structure—as to what is done and when. The congregation cannot sing a hymn while the minister reads the Scripture lesson, nor can the minister preach the sermon while the choir sings an anthem. All must agree to a sequence in the acts of worship, or the result is chaos.

33

Common worship also depends upon our using the same words together. We cannot pray the Lord's Prayer together using different words. One sometimes suspects that we use different tunes in singing our hymns, but we nevertheless need the same words. Christian worship is largely, if not primarily, verbal. This is the case because Christianity is based on historical events, and the memories of such events are transmitted by the use of language. The texts or words which we use must be the same, otherwise we have personal devotions, not common worship.

The third necessity for common worship is that we follow the same actions. The ceremonies in which we engage, some of them half-consciously, must nevertheless be done together. For instance, all stand for the responsive reading, for if some stood, some sat, and some knelt, it would make the responsive reading very nearly impossible as a common *act* of praise. More and more we are coming to see Christian worship as something *done* rather than something absorbed. The imperative "do this" stands behind much of the Christian life, including the work of worship.

Christian common worship results in a disciplined emotion. All worship contains emotion, as we have noted. In personal devotions there is full liberty for its expression. The same kind of liberty is not possible in common worship. Our emotions are still present— otherwise we would be less than human. But they are *disciplined* by the use of the same structure, identical words, and similar actions in order that all present may do their liturgy together. It is a distinct misunderstanding of common worship to try to force the mood of the preacher or any individual (such as a soloist) on the whole congregation. The church does not meet to witness the personal devotions of the minister. Common worship must be a work in which all can engage, not just those who are emotionally attuned to the leader.

It is unfortunate that personal devotions and common worship so often are confused. Both involve distinct discipline. Each is essential in the totality of Christian worship, but each requires a special discipline. Some ministers, feeling that they are being more "liturgical," have simply added more elements of personal devotions to the public service of worship. Unstructured periods of meditation or musical interludes can only remain personal devotions without the discipline which makes such times common worship. Personal devotions should precede the service or follow it, but should not be mixed with it. The other part of Christian worship is the life together expressed in common worship as the church assembles to do its liturgy.

Common worship is a mutual witnessing. In making our offering of praise and thanksgiving we actually are receiving new life. Our giving is receiving, but only when God is the object rather than our "getting something out of worship." Only when God becomes the object and end of worship are the hungry fed.

Finally, it should be remembered that common worship is more than the worship of a single congregation. A congregation is no more isolated from the body of Christ than is an individual worshiper. Whether as individuals following the discipline of personal devotions, or as a congregation acting in the discipline of common worship, we are members of the body of Christ in its corporate worship.

Chapter 2

TWENTY CENTURIES OF CELEBRATION

Christians have been united for almost twenty centuries in their common worship of God. However varied the forms of the worship have been, one thing makes Christian worship possible. This is God's action in history, seen supremely in his giving of himself to men in the form of a man in the time of the first century. Accordingly, Christian worship is not a mystic escape from the world of space and time; it rather is an encounter with the Infinite in and through what he has created. God does not disdain what he has created; in worship, space and time are hallowed as spheres of God's presence.

The history of Christian worship always has involved men's use of what is common to the world—words, actions, and objects. At the very center of the Christian sacraments are such common things as water, bread, and wine joined to such ordinary acts as pouring, breaking, and giving. Men come close to God in worship by using the world in God's service, not by ignoring the world.

As would be expected, the forms of worship change since human life is subject to constant change. Nothing human seems permanent. The course of Christian worship has been changed by such seemingly irrelevant factors as the circumstance that Latin was the native language of Christians in Rome in the third century, but it was not the common language of most people in northern Europe in the thirteenth century. The forms of Christian worship are frequently changed by contingent matters of ordinary human history. In other words, Christian worship is very much of the world in which man lives his life.

But the focus of Christian worship is the eternal, changeless God. In using the changing means of the world in worship, men always are worshiping the same God. Indeed, it is God who makes it possible for men to do their work of worship. Men worship in obedience to God, but it is God who gives men the power to obey. Since it is the Holy Spirit who helps us to worship, the history of Christian worship is part of the story of God's work.

Precisely because God is changeless and eternal he can encounter men in the very fluctuation of our means of worship. Since God remains the same, the forms of worship are not haphazard or by chance. Beneath this apparent diversity they reflect the unchanging nature of the God whom we worship. The amazing fact of the history of Christian worship is not the variety of means of worship but their fundamental unity. The essentials of Christian worship can be discovered in the early church as surely as in the modern church. As one studies the shifting forms of men's worship, one realizes that the unity of our worship rests upon the changeless God whom we worship in common.

The New Testament Church

Reformations in Christian worship have always turned to the New Testament for guidance. In order to understand the worship of the church of the apostolic era, we need to have some idea of the world in the midst of which this worship was celebrated. Christ came into the world, not into a void. The historical situation, the national backgrounds of the early Christians, and their languages had great significance for the forms of their worship. The religious traditions from which the early Christians came left their impressions on the means of worship they used and also prevented the use of other forms. One of our most important statements about the Lord's Supper was written to Christians surrounded by the paganism of Corinth. Doubtless many in the Corinthian church had only recently been engaged in pagan rites. The legacy of Jewish worship was even closer at hand. Yet out of such concrete historical situations emerged many enduring characteristics of Christian worship.

The forms of Jewish worship in the first century inevitably influenced the worship of the church. It must be remembered that Jesus joined in the worship of the Jews. Jewish worship in the Temple, the synagogue, and the home affected Christian worship.

According to Acts, the Christian community in Jerusalem continued to attend the Temple together daily, as they must have done previously as Jews. For several centuries the Temple had been the center of sacrifice in Judaism, and the church early considered its worship a sacrifice. We still speak of our worship as a "sacrifice of praise and thanksgiving." The concept of sacrifice as a means of communion between God and man was not absent from other religions of the first century, and indeed within Judaism it had many aspects. The Letter to the Hebrews compared Christ's sacrifice on the cross with that of the high priest in the earthly Temple.

And in time the concept of sacrifice was specifically connected to the Lord's Supper until Augustine could speak of the whole church as being offered to God in this act through its unity with Christ's offering of himself.

The synagogue provided the focus of Jewish worship throughout the Roman Empire. Its weekly service consisted largely of prayers, the reading of Scripture, preaching, and psalms, basically the ingredients of the normal Protestant Sunday service today. The essence of the service was the commemoration of God's mighty acts on behalf of his people. These acts were recited in worship and praise offered to God for what he had done. At the very center of Jewish life was this coming together to remember those acts of God which had made them a people.

A third area in which the legacy of Jewish worship survived in Christianity was in family worship. This was particularly true of meals which had the character of a sacred occasion. The very act of eating together was a symbol of the union of the participants. Special occasions such as the Passover brought particular historical references and future anticipations to the family meal. It is not strange that Jewish Christians retained the sanctity of the meal, and that Acts considers it worth mentioning that the Jerusalem church both attended the Temple together and broke bread in their homes.

Much more important than the form of any particular service was the strong sense maintained in Judaism of the unity of God's people. The symbol of this, of course, was the covenant which bound God and Israel. The union of God's people, a union always based upon God's initiative, became profoundly deepened in the coming of Christ and the initiation of a "new covenant." Characteristic of the life of the early church was its deep sense of the oneness of those in Christ. We often hear the term "togetherness" today, but what the New Testament describes was no superficial gregariousness. *Oneness,* not togetherness, is the Christian term. This oneness was reflected in two ways. First of all, the Christian was baptized into Christ and joined to his Savior. Secondly, this new relationship inevitably meant he was one with the worshiping community, the church. The Christian community, or *koinonia,* as the Greek word for such a fellowship implied, was one because of its common participation in Christ.

Paul illustrated this oneness with the metaphor of the body of Christ. Just as no part of the human body can survive when detached from the rest of the body, life in Christ meant life in his body. Whether he sees Christ as permeating the entire body or directing it as its head, being in Christ for Paul meant being in his body, the Christian *koinonia.* It is the body of Christ which worships. Indeed the term "church" may first have been applied to the worshiping community. Christian worship is specifically the worship of the body of Christ, and in this sense it is radically different from all other kinds of worship. Much pagan worship focused on the individual and his private concerns; Christian worship is the worship of those who have been made one in Christ. Probably no better symbol of this could be found than in the breaking of bread, when that which is one is shared by all. In worship Christians know their oneness in having received the gifts of God, in their being thrust into community through their acts of worship, and in their anticipation of the fulfillment of God's promises.

No better assurance of the presence of Christ with his people in their worship appeared to the early church than the presence of his spirit as manifested in prophecy and speaking in tongues. Precisely what these acts involved is difficult for us to determine today. But evidently they were understood as praising and glorification of God, and perhaps an intimation of the perfect worship of God as practiced in heaven. The speaking in tongues demanded interpretation for all to understand. And thus, early in its history, we see the beginning of disciplines for common worship. Paul, who excelled in speaking in tongues himself, realized the position of the Christian without this gift who could not very well "say the 'Amen' to your thanksgiving when he does not know what you are saying" (I Cor. 14:16). Paul considered it better to speak five edifying words than ten thousand in a tongue which his fellow worshipers did not understand. The principle, "Let all things be done for edification" (I Cor. 14:26), pointed to the use of forms available to all Christians, but even today the debate continues between established forms and efforts at freedom from forms. Even so, the New Testament itself indicates the use of brief established formulas such as "the Lord is Jesus" and *maranatha* ("Our Lord has come" or "Lord, Come"). Evidence of the use of hymns and other set forms available to all appears in the New Testament.

There are many New Testament references to the practice of baptism by the early Christians, though these glimpses are tantalizing in what they omit. Baptism brought the recipient into a new relationship with Christ and his church. In the act of baptism the church saw a rehearsal of the entire ministry of Jesus, and especially of his death and resurrection. There does seem to be some doubt as to whether the Spirit was recognized as being received in baptism or through a distinct ceremony of the laying on of hands. Frequently both rites may have gone together, followed immediately by first Communion. The new relation to Christ brought a completely new being in uniting one to the church. Paul writes: "For by one Spirit we were all baptized into one body" (I Cor. 12:13), signifying the church. Other interpretations appear: The baptized person has been given new knowledge or received a new birth. Paul stresses the parallel between Christ's death and the death of our former self in baptism by asking: "Do you not know that all of us who have been baptized into Christ Jesus were baptized into his death?" (Rom. 6:3). More is involved than forgiveness of sins—baptism is the entry into a new life in a new body, the church of Christ.

The much-debated question of whether the early church baptized infants can hardly be settled on the basis of the New Testament witness. Judaism used circumcision as the sign that male infants were within the covenant regardless of their own merit, and this may have influenced early Christians to regard baptism of infants as a parallel. Furthermore, there is evidence in Acts 16:15, 33 and I Cor. 1:16 of the baptism of complete households. On the other hand, all the biblical texts concerning baptism deal with adults.

The New Testament contains a number of intriguing references to the Lord's Supper, in addition to the narratives of its institution in the Gospels and I Corinthians. Of these, Paul's account in the tenth and eleventh chapters of I Corinthians is probably the earliest. It is made clear that the sharing of the bread and cup is common participation or communion in Christ. Thus it is both a sharing in Christ and a union with one another through him: "Because there is one loaf, we who are many are one body, for we all partake of the same loaf" (I Cor. 10:17). The actions performed—taking, blessing, breaking, and giving—seem to be as important as the actual bread and wine.

This sacred meal which unites the church looks in two directions. It recalls what the Lord Jesus did "on the night when he was betrayed." But it is also a meal of anticipation "until he comes." The Lukan account looks forward to the time when "you may eat and drink at my table in my kingdom" (22:30). Thus participation in the meal at any time recalls the events of his ministry, his presence with his people throughout history, and the messianic banquet in his kingdom.

At an early time, possibly within the first century, the breaking of bread was connected with the first day of the week (Acts 20:7). Evidently for some time it was a full meal with the command of

Christ to "do this" attached specifically to the acts connected with the bread and wine. Paul indicates that this meal often degenerated into gluttony, and there was probably within New Testament times a division between the sacred meal of the Lord's Supper and an actual meal, the love feast (Jude 12), a service recovered by John Wesley. It is important to remember that the Lord's Supper was celebrated for those who were already within the body of Christ. Thus, whenever it was celebrated, it was a sacrament of the unity which existed between the believers and their Lord.

The Early Church

In recent years we have come to know much more about the worship of the early church, though large gaps in our knowledge still remain. The conditions under which Christians worshiped during the second and third centuries of the Christian Era certainly had great consequences for their manner of worship. During much of this time Christianity was a forbidden religion, frequently under persecution. Often this meant that Christians assembled for common worship at the risk of their lives. Only an earnest Christian would risk his life to join in such activity as Christian common worship. Yet the amazing fact of this period is the persistency with which Christians maintained their worship together.

These furtive groups, worshiping in secret, were united by the closest of bonds—their oneness in Christ. There was no room here for the lukewarm Christian who might, in a moment of fear, betray the church. The requirements for admission to the worship of the church included a strenuous period of training and preparation. This was climaxed in baptism, the laying on of hands, and admission to Communion. Not until he had been examined and baptized could the new believer join with the church in prayers of intercession and in receiving Communion.

The person who passed through the rites of Christian initiation in these early centuries became a member of a community which increasingly was following definite customs in its worship. About the middle of the second century, a Roman Christian by the name of Justin (later to witness to his faith with his life) wrote a description of Christian worship as he knew it. From the details he gives it is possible to gather that the service Justin knew followed a fairly well-established pattern. But the wording had not yet congealed; the presiding Christian offered prayers "according to his ability." The tendency to usage of traditional forms increased as time progressed. Sometime near the end of the second century or the beginning of the third (ca. A.D. 200), a Roman minister by the name of Hippolytus felt compelled to write out the form of the Eucharist for the better guidance of the contemporary Bishop of Rome. At this early date (more than seventeen hundred years ago) we find phrases still echoed in our own Holy Communion. "Lift up your hearts," the bishop says, and the people reply, "We lift them up unto the Lord." The dialogue continues, now as then: "Let us give thanks unto the Lord," and the people reply, "It is meet and right."

By the third century Christian worship seems to have coalesced into two patterns, the Service of the Word and the Eucharist (as the Holy Communion was often called, from the Greek word for thanksgiving). The Service of the Word is reflected in the usual Sunday service of most American Protestants. Its roots are in the worship of the synagogue, the gathering of God's people to commemorate God's acts and to praise him for them. Basically it consists of prayers, reading from the Scriptures (both Old Testament and New), psalms or hymns, and a sermon. The catechumens (those who were preparing to become Christians) were often allowed to attend this part of the service, but usually were dismissed at its conclusion when the Eucharist followed. The most important occasion for the Service of the Word was Sunday morning, when it preceded the Eucharist.

The Service of the Word also led to another development. Christians and Jews had long engaged in specified occasions of prayer and the reading of Scripture, both in private and together. Hippolytus encouraged Christians to pray upon rising and at the equivalents of nine, noon, three, upon going to bed, and at midnight. By the end of the fourth century specified patterns of prayer and scripture reading had become common. These services found their greatest development among the monastics and the clergy. They became known as the choir offices, since eventually the services were usually said in the chancels of churches. In some religious orders there were seven daily offices and a night office. Worship became the most important work of the monastics. These choir offices consisted of scripture lessons, psalms, canticles, and prayers. Essentially they could be said by any Christian, but in practice they came to be more and more the work of the monastics and clergy. It is the Service of the Word as developed through the choir offices which largely forms the contents of the usual Protestant Sunday service today.

Although the Eucharist was celebrated in all parts of the Christian world, there was an amazing degree of consistency in the shape of the liturgy. By the fourth century the Service of the Word had generally developed into a standard form: greeting, lesson, psalm, lesson, sermon, dismissal of catechumens, and prayers. When the Eucharist was also celebrated, it too followed accustomed patterns throughout almost all of Christendom. In *The Shape of The Liturgy* Gregory Dix speaks of four actions which the liturgical tradition reproduces "with absolute unanimity." These acts are the *taking* of the elements in an offertory, *giving* thanksgiving for them in form of prayer, *breaking* the bread that it might be distributed, and the *giving* of the Communion to God's people. It is interesting to compare this primitive shape of the liturgy with present-day communion services. Many of these basic forms and actions are common throughout Christendom, and it seems presumptuous to ignore them without good reason.

During the fourth century the status of Christianity changed from that of an illegal religion to one tolerated and even maintained by the Empire. The consequences for worship were great, especially as the newly respectable faith found thousands of new adherents. From a persecuted sect to the religion of the Empire was a mighty transition. Sumptuous churches were constructed and the wealth of the Empire lavished on their ornamentation. To the simplicity of Christian worship was added the splendor of court ceremony. Under Constantine the center of the Empire had moved to the East and the etiquette of oriental potentates found its way into the worship of the church. In this great new respectability and prosperity much of the intimacy of the small and persecuted liturgical assembly was lost.

Yet even today, the liturgy of the great eastern Orthodox churches (represented in America by such groups as the Greek Orthodox Church and the Russian Orthodox Church) reflects the period of persecution in an exclamation about guarding the doors. Indeed, Orthodox worship has changed little in more than a thousand years. Western Christians, Protestant and Roman Catholic alike, have come to a new appreciation of Orthodox worship, which in its conservatism has preserved a rather different spirit from that which typifies worship in the West.

No service in Christendom better expresses a sense of awe and mystery than that of the Eastern Christians. Indeed, so awesome is much of the liturgy that the priest performs parts of it behind a screen which shields the worshipers from the holy mysteries. The very church building itself represents heaven. The dome and walls of the church are covered with paintings of the saints in heaven with whose worship the church on earth joins. The service is joyful in tone, for Christ has triumphed over death and his own are with him in heaven. Though the congregation has lost its direct participation in most of the acts of the liturgy, it nevertheless retains a strong communal sense of participation in the worship of heaven. The oneness of the church on earth and in heaven is rehearsed every time the Orthodox churches perform the liturgy.

Medieval Christianity

In Western Europe the worship of medieval Catholicism underwent a gradual transformation. For part of the medieval period several different liturgies were in use throughout the West, though the differences were not nearly so great as the basic similarities. Charlemagne did his best to introduce a standardized form of saying Mass throughout his empire. It was based on that in use in Rome, but the emendations of the great eight-century scholar Alcuin, replete with prayers and rubrics popular in the North, came to be part of the Mass, and in turn found their way back to Rome. Still it was not until the time of the Reformation that Roman Catholicism effectively enforced a single uniform text for the Mass.

Worship in Western Christendom came to have certain characteristics which distinguished it somewhat from the worship of Eastern Christians. In brief, the West tended to concentrate on the sufferings of Christ and the unworthiness of men for whom he suffered, with the crucifix taking the place in Western churches reserved for symbols of Christ in glory in Eastern churches. Devotions to the sorrowful mysteries were reflected in an obsession with men's unworthiness, and the rather subjective element of confession dominated Western piety in contrast with the joyful praise of God in Eastern worship.

47

Western Christianity cultivated a much more literal sense of calendar time than the Orthodox. The Mass has numerous elements which change to match the date in the Christian year. Medieval Christianity saw the elaboration of the Christian year in seasons and special days of commemoration. The Christian year originally began with the high festival of Easter, succeeded by "the great fifty days," a period of exultation lasting until Pentecost. The period before Easter had been a period of preparation, as converts from pagan religions were instructed in the faith and anticipated baptism during the Easter vigil. Largely through historical factors, especially the tragedies of barbarian invasions of Christendom, Lent became a penitential season. The Good Friday observance became detached from Easter and focused upon devotions to the Cross. Pentecost seems to have been as ancient a season in Christanity as Easter and in Judiasm referred back to the giving of the covenant at Mount Sinai. Christmas was added eventually as another great festival. Other seasons found their way into the calendar, especially Advent, Christmastide, and Epiphany. Over the course of many centuries the calendar became cluttered with commemorations of saints both famous and obscure, and even such events as Adam's birthday (March 23).

Such elaboration of the calendar was perhaps a symptom of what was happening to much of Western worship in the Middle Ages. As the calendar became more and more complex, it became necessary to write out directions and finally even a book to help the priest find the proper parts of the service for the day. Since few of the laity could read, their role in worship was increasingly transformed. Even after the Christianizing of northern Europe was complete, the service remained in Latin, a language alien to most of the people. It was hard enough educating the priests so that they could read the Mass and follow the rubrics; it was impossible to train the laity to understand the words of the Mass. The choir offices were the same—monastics and clergy said their offices in a language meaningless to most people.

Gradually the priest and his worship became detached from the congregation. The altar was removed from its position before the congregation to the further end of a long chancel rarely entered by a layman who did not belong to a religious order. The crucifix on the altar became the center of the priest's devotions and he frequently said Mass without a congregation. Even when a congregation was present the people rarely received Communion more frequently than once a year, and in the late Middle Ages they only partook of the bread.

The laity were not idle, although they were deprived of any active participation in the Mass now no longer visible or audible to them. They occupied themselves in a series of devotions, saying the rosary, meditating upon the sufferings of Christ, and venerating relics of the saints. These devotions were not part of the liturgy; their whole reference was to the individual and his own salvation.

The legacy of medieval developments was not entirely erased by the Reformation. In the Middle Ages the corporate sense of worship by the entire body of Christ through common acts, words, and structures gradually became obscured. It was replaced by a religious individualism rather than a sense of the oneness of those engaged in common worship. The clergy acted as if they were the church and the laity ceased to do most of their proper work in common worship. This clericalism was a far cry from the worship of the New Testament period.

The Reformation

It was to the New Testament and the early church that the Protestant Reformers of the sixteenth century tried to return. So many theological issues were at stake in the Reformation, that it is often forgotten that it was largely a movement of liturgical renewal. Matters of worship were central issues throughout the Reformation. Unfortunately, the Reformers knew much less about the worship of the New Testament and the early church than we do today. But there can be no mistaking the sincere desire of many of them to return to early forms of worship. At times they carried this to excesses of legalism while protesting at the same time against the idolatry of others.

The Reformation was characterized by the rediscovery of the church as the whole people of God. This had radical implications for worship. It meant that once again the laity were called to do their work in worship, to perform their own liturgy rather than being passive spectators or engaging in their own personal devotions during common worship. Essentially it meant that the ministry of the laity was rediscovered. Luther expressed this as the priesthood of all believers. The whole church, laity and clergy alike, were ministers to one another. And this was supremely true of worship where all performed their work together in God's presence.

In order to recover a corporate sense in common worship, certain drastic changes were necessitated in the forms of worship received from the medieval church. The Reformers felt compelled to translate the services into a language understood by the people. It was obviously too much to expect the laity to engage actively in worship in a language they did not understand. Various expedients were taken to make the service visible, such as placing the altar table before the people in the nave and even closing off the chancels. Many of the Reformers stressed the importance of frequent Communion, sometimes with the hope that the laity would receive Communion weekly. As might be expected, they agreed that everyone was to receive both bread and wine. In some places the singing of hymns and psalms and congregational prayers were introduced in order that the laity could take an active part in worship.

The Reformers were never fully successful in recapturing either the spirit or the forms of worship in the early church. After all, the Reformers were products of sixteen centuries of Christian tradition, and specifically of the Western tradition. The Passion of Christ still remained the focus of Protestant piety as it had in Roman Catholicism. Much of the individualism of late medieval Catholicism persisted within Protestantism. Though the corporate life of the church was manifested in much of Protestant worship, it generally lacked the intensity which it had had in the early church.

The failures of the Reformers are instructive. Though Luther, Calvin, and Cranmer desired to have the laity communicate weekly, this was too radical a change from the practice of yearly communion then current. In the Church of England, for example, morning and evening prayer came to be the normal Sunday services rather than Holy Communion. It was not until the time of Wesley that frequent Communion was achieved. Furthermore, the laity did not take as active a part in the service as desired. It may be that the history of Christian worship is the history of human laziness; certainly Protestantism has reduplicated the professionalization of worship by clergy and choir, much as happened in the Middle Ages. Basically, the Reformers of the sixteenth century added little to the traditions of Christian worship. Instead, they purged those items which they considered wrong.

Having said this much, it is important to realize the great contributions the Reformers did succeed in making. They rediscovered the importance of the Service of the Word, with its focus on the Scriptures and their exposition in preaching. As Calvin put it in his *Institutes:* "Whether we are to be confirmed in faith, or exercised in confession, or aroused to duty, there is need of preaching." With the lessons in a language understood by the people and preaching helping to interpret them, the importance of the Bible in

51

the life of the laity was stressed. Furthermore, all the people could join in proclamation and praise by the use of hymns and psalms. As the services were made intelligible and audible the congregations participated in common worship to a much greater degree than they had in the Middle Ages.

Each of the great Reformers made special contributions to worship. Luther tended to be conservative in many ways, feeling that the abuse of many practices did not mean that their use was to be abolished absolutely. Thus Luther could retain many of the ceremonial practices of the Middle Ages but could be ruthless in excising those portions of the Mass which he found theologically contrary to his ideas. From Luther stems the great appreciation of hymns and preaching so characteristic of Protestant worship. Zwingli, Luther's contemporary in Switzerland, was more radical in many ways. Zwingli purged the services of many elements, seeking a form of worship which was eminently intelligible. In the absence of traditional symbols a fine austerity developed with a high sense of union in the faith professed together.

Calvin, the Genevan reformer, taught a profound understanding of the importance of the church for the elect, and the unity of preaching and the Holy Communion, both being vital to those in the invisible church. His ideas had great significance throughout English-speaking Protestantism, most obviously among Presbyterians, but strongly in the Anglican, Puritan, and Methodist traditions as well. The Anabaptists, partly because of extensive persecution, developed a strong sense of the suffering church and achieved an intense realization of community in worship. Though they varied in the forms of their worship, some demanding no forms at all, they did concur in reserving baptism for those who were old enough to profess their faith.

The Reformation in England was led by Archbishop Thomas Cranmer. His knowledge of liturgics and his literary abilities helped to produce the Book of Common Prayer, which has guided the worship of Anglicans and many Protestants for more than four centuries. As its name indicates, the Book of Common Prayer (like the Scottish *Book of Common Order*) intended to restore common worship by enabling the laity to take their part. Cranmer reduced the choir offices to two (morning prayer and evening prayer) in which the laity could participate actively. He translated the Mass, removing a few objectionable items and encouraging frequent Communion.

Not all Englishmen were satisfied with the Book of Common Prayer. Eventually, the Puritans argued that it yet retained many items for which there was no biblical sanction. They attempted further purifications by removing many ceremonies. The austerity of Puritan worship focused on receiving the Word of God in preaching and in sacrament, with complete concentration on what they regarded as essential. Preaching increasingly came to be the keynote of Puritan worship, and their services probably suffered from a tendency toward being overly educational. The most radical type of Protestant worship developed among the Quakers. They eliminated all outward forms. But their effort was directed at achieving a truly corporate worship from the witness of the Holy Spirit delivered to the entire congregation through an individual "speaking from the group." The gathered meeting of the Quakers deliberately avoids individualism such as "speaking from one's self" in favor of a corporate waiting upon God.

Methodist Worship

The Methodist movement in the eighteenth century was in some ways a completion of the Reformation of the sixteenth century. It united many of the themes of the earlier Reformation and accomplished some of the intentions of the Reformers. Most immediately it united elements of the Anglican and Puritan traditions.

John and Charles Wesley both remained priests of the Church of England until their deaths. They had grown up in the tradition of the Book of Common Prayer, and it remained their constant companion. When late in his life John Wesley prepared a prayer-book for American Methodists, he simply revised the Book of Common Prayer, saying that he knew of none "of a more solid, scriptural, rational piety than the Common Prayer of the Church of England." Within the Anglican Church the Wesleys continued the high-church tradition, particularly in their emphasis on a discipline of worship with its center in the Holy Communion. It was this, in large measure, which earned them the name "Methodist."

Indeed, the Wesleys far outdid the Church of England of the time in their stress on frequent Communion. In most Anglican churches of the time, Holy Communion was rarely celebrated more than three or four times a year. By his preaching John Wesley urged "that it is the duty of every Christian to receive the Lord's Supper as often as he can." By his example he practiced this precept, often receiving Communion twice a week. The theology of the Wesleys stressed the presence of Christ in the sacrament and his benefits which the Holy Spirit confirms in the believers. The Wesleys' hymns show a very profound understanding of the sacrament.

On the other hand, John Wesley developed a pragmatic willingness to adapt worship to practical necessities. The result occasionally was a much more nearly apostolic practice than the traditions of his church allowed, and John Wesley ventured beyond the canon law of the Church of England. This became particularly evident in his field preaching whenever he could draw an audience and in building preaching-houses for Methodist worship. It should be remembered that Methodist services were intended to supplement the worship of the Anglican parish church. The Methodist services brought the possibility of more preaching and extempore prayer. There was a conscious desire in the Methodist societies to obtain a disciplined life, and common worship became a major element in this. The class meetings especially strengthened this desire for discipline. Special services were developed for the Methodist people. Wesley adapted the love feast of the Moravians (and of the early church) as a symbolic meal with prayer, praise, and offering of personal witness. The Moravian watch-night services became monthly occasions of "singing, praying, and praising God" among Methodists. Wesley adapted the dramatic covenant service from the Presbyterian tradition.

No survey of Methodist worship would be complete without mention of Methodist hymnody. Although it had been anticipated by the Congregational hymn writer, Isaac Watts, the Wesleys made hymn singing an important part of worship among English-speaking Protestants. Within a century Anglicans and almost all Protestants had made hymns an important part of their worship. Many of the Wesleyan hymns are paraphrases of theological treatises with objective doctrinal fundations. Yet they contain a catholicity which appeals to Christians beyond the bounds of Protestantism. John Wesley seems to have had a negative attitude toward anthems in services of common worship, but readily welcomed hymn singing as the proper work of the whole people of God.

Eighteenth-century Methodism was in a real sense a liturgical renewal. Under John Wesley's guidance, the two halves of Christian worship, the Service of the Word and the Eucharist, received a balance rarely surpassed in the history of Protestant worship. The importance of the Word heard in preaching and the Word visible in the sacrament were both recognized and successfully made a part of Methodist worship. Christian groups since that time have tended to emphasize one or the other. The witness to both in eighteenth-century Methodism is an important contribution to the ecumenical movement of our day as well as to contemporary Methodism. In accomplishing this balance, Wesley actually succeeded in achieving that which Luther, Calvin, and Cranmer had attempted, but which their traditions had failed to attain or to preserve.

The Nineteenth Century

The last century was of great significance for Protestant worship since it marked the real watershed between the period of the Reformation and the present. As far as worship was concerned, the nineteenth century succeeded in reversing many of the trends of the Reformation, though frequently at the same time professing its loyalty to the spirit of the Reformers. Most Protestant worship today strongly reflects the concepts of the nineteenth century.

Paradoxically, some of the trends in the nineteenth century which directly affected worship were diametrically opposite in most of their characteristics but similar in their total effect. Two of these movements can be called, for lack of better terms, Revivalism and Romanticism.

Revivalism was one of the most important factors in making America a Christian nation, and in the process it made a significant impact on Christian worship, especially by developing one aspect of it and neglecting much of the rest. American Revivalism derived many of its characteristics from the frontier camp meeting. On these occasions pioneers gathered for several days to hear preaching by members of different denominations. The emphasis was on winning souls to Christ, and this was conceived of largely in individualistic terms. The hymns growing out of the camp meeting background are largely descriptive of individual religious experience.

In time, the measures so effective on the frontier were brought into the mainstream of Protestantism in the more settled areas as well as on the frontier. One of the consequences of Revivalism was that it very nearly reduced the importance of the church to being only a means of continuing the promotion of revivals. The zeal of Revivalism was directed to the salvation of individuals, and once they were converted they were usually directed to various reform crusades often organized as benevolent societies with no direct connection to any church. The church tended to be treated as an option rather than the body of Christ in which God's people found their oneness. Worship was highly colored by this attitude. Increasingly it was regarded as a means to an end—the conversion of the unconverted—rather than as an end in itself.

The setting of one form of Romanticism could hardly have been more different. It appeared as a result of a movement begun by a group of fellows of Oxford University in England. The name Oxford Movement, or Tractarianism, is often given to the resulting theological revolution. Foremost in the thinking of the Tractarians were high concepts of the church and the sacraments. Unfortunately, their high doctrine of the church frequently turned out in practice to be a high doctrine of the ministry. They did have considerable success in recovering frequent Communion, a practice which had hardly outlived John Wesley in Methodism.

While the Oxford scholars were not particularly affected by Romanticism, their disciples at Cambridge University were heavily influenced by it. From the Cambridge Movement came the changes in worship reflecting the changes in theology championed at Oxford. The Cantabrigians had very romantic conceptions of the worship of the Middle Ages, and overlooked its debilitating individualism. They set out to recapture the splendor of medieval worship, and the most obvious means which occurred to them was to build churches in Gothic architecture with the divided chancel and ornaments of the fourteenth century. They welcomed the clericalism which this implied and succeeded, despite strenuous persecution, in restoring much of the ceremonial of medieval Christian wor-

57

ship. Many of these ornaments and ceremonies have since found their way into all the major Protestant denominations.

One of the prime purposes in the restoration of medieval architecture was to stimulate a feeling of reverence and mystery. This so-called worshipful atmosphere had obvious advantages, but it tended to suggest that worship was primarily a private and subjective matter. It further enforced individualism in worship. At the same time, clergy and choir came to dominate most of the service, since their performance was obviously aesthetically superior to that of the untrained congregation. Holy Communion tended to be a special weekly service at an early hour for the saints in the congregation who cared enough to get up early and attend. But even here the concept of the worshiping church in which the entire body of Christ gathered to do its common worship suffered. Frequent Communion was largely treated as an ascetic ideal in Anglican circles, rather than as the norm of worship.

Revivalism and Romanticism did much to heighten individualism in worship, and led to a serious attrition of the idea of worship as a common act of obedience. There is an ironic parallel in this, since the same thing had happened in medieval worship when the laity had turned to their private devotions when they no longer played an active part in the Mass. Something very similar happened in the nineteenth century and still colors much of Protestant worship today.

The Modern Liturgical Movement

In our own time one of the most profound renewals of common worship is occurring. Surprisingly enough it crosses lines between Roman Catholicism and Protestantism. It poses greatest hope for better mutual understanding and closer union of Christendom.

The liturgical movement in Roman Catholicism is working the most drastic revolution within that branch of Christianity in centuries. Had what is happening today happened in the fifteenth century instead, the Reformation might have taken place within Catholicism, without any schism. Most of this transformation has taken place in the twentieth century. Indeed, sixteenth-century Catholicism attempted to preserve most medieval tendencies in worship, and in the following centuries even more cults, devotions, and festivals were added to the medieval accumulation. There was, however, more attention to making the Mass visible, and the adoration of Christ in the service of benediction became a very popular devotion.

Early in the twentieth century Pope Pius X urged the laity to receive Communion frequently (as anticipated by Wesley) and to pray the Mass rather than their own private devotions during it. Since then there has been a major rediscovery of the laity and their part in the worship of the church. It has been realized by many that for the laity to take their part in worship they must be theologically literate. Liturgy has often been referred to as the theology of the laity. They must know their faith explicitly rather than simply be satisfied with an implicit trust that the church guards the truth. This tendency has led to a great revival in biblical study among the Catholic laity, an innovation which has profound consequences for church unity.

Concrete evidence of the liturgical movement is lacking in many areas of Catholicism, partly due to conservatism and partly because of the embarrassing fact that the Protestant Reformers made the obvious correction in many instances. Yet the Second Vatican Council is evidence of how far have come the crusades for having the Mass in a popular language, the elimination of personal devotions from the churches during Mass, celebration facing the people, and other means of engaging the people in the Mass. New concepts centering around the acts in the Mass have raised important new theological questions about the sacrament. There is real concern in some parts of Roman Catholicism to recover the corporate sense of the common worship of the early church as the Protestant Reformers tried to do.

Within Protestantism the liturgical movement has gained much ground in the last quarter century, though its gains have been scattered and have left no impact on large areas of Protestantism, especially in this country. Wherever it has gone it has been a companion of the great theological revolution now occurring in Protestantism. Indeed, the liturgical movement is theological through and through; and where theology is ignored, the movement has made only superficial progress, if any. A large part of modern theological currents are concerned with a new biblical theology which deals very seriously with the strong emphasis on the covenant community in the Old and New Testaments. The ecumenical movement has led Protestants to deal seriously with the problems of ministry and sacraments which divide us. In delving into these problems, all denominations have rediscovered their own traditions, often finding their own current reflections of them almost unrecognizable. In many instances this has led to a reaffirmation of the central tenets of the Reformation. Consequently, both the aims and failures of the Reformers have profoundly influenced Protestant theology today.

Some of the first stirrings of the Protestant liturgical movement appeared in the Church of England. This was partly under the prompting of contemporary theology, but partly no doubt due to the fact that in sections of England Christians have become a minority. This has forced churchmen to seek the essentials of Christianity, something not always easily done when the church is full of successful organizations. In a number of cases the consequence has been a rediscovery of the worship of the whole congregation in a single service, the Parish Communion. Here the emphasis is on the gathering of the whole people of God, with all taking their active part in the liturgy. On the other hand, there has been a renewed interest in holding the services of the church in private homes during the week, with all gathering in the parish church for the one great service on Sunday morning. At the same time there has been a new realization of the importance of preaching and the need of the Word both preached and made visible. Where the liturgical movement has moved, it has made the old terms "high church" and "low church" irrelevant, for the participants are merely seeking to be faithful to the spirit of the New Testament and in so doing often pass the Reformation on the way. The liturgical movement has made progress in some Protestant denominations in this country, in Europe, and in the younger churches of Africa and Asia.

The question must be raised as to how much impact the liturgical movement has made on American Methodism. As yet it is very little in evidence. The reasons for this can be shown by a bit of historical reflection. As Methodists—and many other Protestants— entered the twentieth century, their advancing education and sophistication tended to discard the emotionalism of nineteenth-century worship. But the same stress on feeling in worship persisted under the guise of aestheticism. Here the impact of Romanticism, especially the Cambridge Movement, came into full flower. Methodists built large Gothic churches, decorating them with all kinds of art, sometimes of great quality. The bent of all this was upon producing a worshipful atmosphere in which a worshipful experience could be felt. There was an interest in the psychology of worship, as people sought means for producing worshipful experiences. Worship was considered primarily as a matter of feeling rather than as a work of obedience. The idea became common that one worshiped to get something out of it rather than that one offered worship to God; and in giving, received.

The question now before Methodism and much of American Protestantism is whether it will immerse itself in the theological movements of our time and thus make a genuine liturgical movement possible within Methodism, or whether it will remain aloof. In moving into contemporary theological currents, with their strong emphasis on the holiness of God—the God made known by his acts in history for his people whom he has joined to himself in community—Methodism would be moving closer to John Wesley himself. Without a theologically concerned laity and clergy, Methodism can never really participate in the liturgical movement. The new revisions of *The Methodist Hymnal* and *The Book of Worship* give some evidence that already Methodism is moving in this direction. Only time can tell how close we are to our foundations.

Chapter 3

THE WHOLENESS OF THE CELEBRATION

We have found that in speaking of Christian worship we must use such terms as "life in Christ," "the body of Christ," "the victory of God through Jesus Christ." Obviously, the meaning of Jesus Christ is the heart of all that we are saying about Christian worship. Apart from him, Christian worship is impossible. Let us now consider the meaning of Jesus Christ, and the way in which the church may insure that her worship is the celebration of the whole gospel of our Lord.

The purpose of God is the way that we might best come at the meaning of Jesus Christ. "For God so loved the world that [as a consequence of his love] he gave his only Son, that [for the purpose that] whoever believes in him should not perish but have eternal life." (John 3:16.) "He destined us in love to be his sons through

Jesus Christ, according to the purpose of his will." (Eph. 1:5.) "In him, according to the purpose of him who accomplishes all things according to the counsel of his will, we who first hoped in Christ have been destined and appointed to live for the praise of his glory." (Eph. 1:11-12.) Jesus Christ is the one through whom God has chosen to bring about his purpose for us and for all men.

The purposeful action of God in Christ is called the gospel, which is "good news." But "good news" is really good news only when it means something of importance to the one to whom it comes. It is good news to a man in prison when he learns that he has been pardoned; to the accused in court, when he hears the judge say "not guilty"; to a father when he is assured that his critically ill son will recover; to a nation, when it receives word that a war is over. The gospel is "good news" to us if it comes as deliverance from imprisonment, guilt, death, and conflict—if it means that we are redeemed into a restored relationship to God.

This is why the first chapter of the gospel story sketches the account of creation in a few grand, brisk strokes, and carries us at once into the lostness of man's broken responsiveness to God. The gospel of the Redeemer has meaning for those who know their need to be redeemed from death to life, from lostness to foundness, from sin to righteousness, from aloneness to community, from hatred to love, from fear to assurance, from meaninglessness to hope. To them the gospel is the desperately needed and joyfully received "good news."

The gospel story, then, largely is that of God's purposeful action to redeem his lost people. Throughout the history of Israel, God moved to effect his purpose with his covenant people: through law-givers, judges, kings, and prophets. At last he took the strange action of coming to man himself through his Son, who though one with the Father became one with us, taking our nature upon himself and sharing our condition of humanity; living among us as teacher, healer, and preacher; being crucified for our sins; being raised up by the power of the Father; ascending into heaven to be Lord and Judge; sending the Holy Spirit to be "God among us," prompting us to be members of the community of faith, love, and hope until his coming again, to complete in fullness the victory of God that was established in principle by his first coming.

Such is the "bare-bones" outline of the early church's witness to the gospel—to God's victory. However strange to us in this twentieth century may be the sound of this gospel story in biblical language, it remains the basic way in which we have to talk about the purpose of God in Jesus Christ. It is right that we should use as many present-day thought forms, analogies, and paraphrases as we can to make clear the meaning of the gospel, but we cannot really get away from biblical language in our worship. However stated, we always are left with the fact that the gospel means that God's purpose is the determining reference of all things, that we are dependent upon him, and that his action through Jesus Christ and the Holy Spirit is definitive for the meaning and hope of our lives.

There is no way that we can know the gospel without mystery. A mystery is vital, living, self-contained truth, differing in kind from ordinary fact and incapable of being broken down into parts. To attempt to reduce the gospel to "everyday common sense"— that is, something that we can understand in the same way we understand everything else—is to try to make of the gospel a set of ideas that we undertake to comprehend as we do other ideas. But there is mystery in God that cannot be comprehended. There is mystery in God the Holy Trinity. There is mystery in Jesus Christ in his oneness with God and with us. He is indeed "God's mystery, . . . in whom are hid all the treasures of wisdom and knowledge" (Col. 2:2-3). "Great indeed, we confess, is the mystery of our religion."

> He was manifested in the flesh,
> vindicated in the spirit,
>   seen by angels,
> preached among the nations,
> believed on in the world,
>   taken up in glory.
>   —I Tim. 3:16

It is ours to enter into the mystery with the understanding that is living faith, not just accepting the mystery as something that we must blindly believe, but responding to it in the way that means a participation in the victory that God has prepared for us. "For he has made known to us in all wisdom and insight the mystery of his will, according to his purpose which he set forth in Christ as a plan for the fullness of time, to unite all things in him, things in heaven and things on earth." (Eph. 1:9-10.)

The Wholeness of Jesus Christ

Let us now consider the wholeness of Jesus Christ. The whole meaning of Jesus Christ so defies a simple putting that he is called by more than fifty names in the New Testament, some of which are: Jesus; the Son of Joseph; the Son of Mary; Rabbi; Teacher; Master; Prophet; Christ; Jesus Christ; Lord Jesus Christ; Our Savior Christ Jesus; the Son of David; the Son of Man; the Servant; the Lord; the Son of God; the Only Begotten Son; the King; He That Cometh; the Holy One; the Righteous One; the Judge; the Lion of the Tribe of Judah; the Root and Offspring of David; the Bright and Morning Star; He That Hath the Key of David; the Bridegroom; the Shepherd; the Author; the Pioneer; the Stone;

the Head of the Body; the True Vine; the Saviour; the Mediator; the High Priest; the Lamb; the Expiation; the Image of God; the Radiance of the Divine Glory; the Light of the World; the Bread of Life; the Door of the Sheep; the Resurrection and the Life; the Way, and the Truth, and the Life; the Firstborn; the Power and the Wisdom of God; the Last Adam; Alpha and Omega; the First and the Last; the Beginning and the End; the Beloved; the Word; and the Amen.[1]

For our purposes we will concentrate upon the meaning of Jesus Christ as contained in the basic preaching of the early church.

This primal proclamation of the gospel included reference to the Lord's pre-existence with God (John 1:1-5), his virgin birth, his obedient life, his passion, his crucifixion, his resurrection, his ascension, the sending of the Holy Spirit, and his coming again.

Any time that we speak of "Jesus Christ," we speak of the One of whom all this is true at once.

Pre-existence. The pre-existence of Jesus Christ pertains to his eternal divinity—to his unity with God before his earthly life, as well as during and after. It signifies that the Redeemer and the Creator are one in being and purpose. The one whom we call "Savior" was with God from the beginning, and "through him all things were made."

Virgin Birth. The Virgin Birth is the gospel story way of saying that Jesus Christ is both divine and human. It emphasizes the humanity of Jesus Christ fully as much as it does his divinity. This is the doctrine of the Incarnation, of course; that is, that Jesus Christ on earth was God-in-flesh—in human form. It is not the miracle of unique birth that is of primary importance here, but the mystery of the divine-human nature of Jesus Christ.

The Obedient Life. The obedient life of Jesus Christ is his unfailing responsiveness to the purpose of God while he was here on

[1] See Vincent Taylor, *The Names of Jesus* (New York: St. Martin's Press, 1953).

earth. In his work of teaching, healing, and preaching and in his personal associations, Jesus Christ represented all mankind in his single devotion to the Father. His prayer in the garden, "Not my will, but thine, be done," catches up the completeness of his obedience, for it was obedience even unto death, if need be.

The Passion. The Passion of Jesus Christ is his at-oneness with men in suffering on their behalf. If Jesus Christ were wholly divine and not at all human, his suffering for man would indeed be astounding, but it would not have achieved the redemptive transformation of human nature.

The Crucifixion and Resurrection. The Crucifixion and Resurrection must be seen separately and together. Crucifixion alone is the stark, unlimited extent to which men went in their sin and to which Jesus Christ went for our sake. It is definite and actual, and we do well not to hurry from the Crucifixion to the Resurrection in such a way that crucifixion is passed by, dismissed, or modified as temporary and therefore unreal. The Resurrection is the definitive action of the purposeful power of God. In some prayers of consecration in the service of Holy Communion, it is called the *"mighty* Resurrection." It is the declarative work of God that nothing—not even death—will at last thwart his purpose to redeem his people. If we were starting with the heart of the gospel to which all else necessarily is related, we might well start with the Resurrection. The Resurrection does not have meaning when standing alone, but it is a sort of high center to which all else relates—that which comes before and that which comes after. Crucifixion-resurrection seen from the afterside, is the one great two-movement transaction of redemption—the down-into-death and up-into-life, the dying to the old self and being raised up to the new self in Christ. (Rom. 6:3-4.)

The Ascension. The Ascension is the mystery that signifies the present and eternal lordship of Jesus Christ. "He ascended into

heaven, and sitteth at the right hand of God the Father Almighty"
is the "worship way" of saying, "Jesus Christ is Lord." The purely
divine Son who came into the world by the loving purpose of the
Father to save us by taking our nature upon himself, has returned
to the Father to be henceforth perfectly human as well as perfectly
divine. Whereas he came as the representative of God's redemptive
love to us, he has returned to be also the representative of our
redeemed nature to the Father. This is why we pray, "through
Jesus Christ our Lord." We pray through our Lord and Savior
who as *Savior* is our representative to God.

The Descent of the Holy Spirit. The descent of the Holy Spirit—
the coming of the Counselor sent by the Father in the name of
the ascended Lord (John 14:16)—is a continuation of the redemptive purpose of God. Jesus Christ ascended and the Holy Spirit
descended. God is yet with us! The victory that God had established
in principle through the Crucifixion, Resurrection, and Ascension
of the Incarnate Christ is made specific in our hearts by the Holy
Spirit. God's redemptive work goes on! That which the Holy
Spirit does is at one with "the meaning of Jesus Christ"; and the
meaning of Jesus Christ is at one with the purpose of God. This is
"the Word." The Word is the loving purpose of God the sovereign
Father that was revealed in God the Son, made known and secured
to us by God the Holy Spirit. "The Word," then, always means
the effectual action of the one God, Father, Son, and Holy Spirit.
Even so, we may say that we now are living in the age of the
Holy Spirit. That is, by the gospel reckoning of time, we are
between the comings of Jesus Christ, his first coming and his
second coming. During this age, the Holy Spirit is the active
presence of God, carrying on the redemptive purpose of God that
he established in and through Jesus Christ. (John 14:16-17, 26;
15:26.)

The Coming Again. The coming again means that God the Sovereign will complete victoriously what he has set out to do through Jesus Christ. It is regrettable that excesses concerning the second coming (distorted interpretations of Daniel, Ezekiel, Thessalonians, Revelation; the setting of the date for the end of the world; lurid and repelling pictures and literature) have caused some Christians to avoid any mention of this essential and powerful Christian doctrine. As a matter of fact, there is no way to preach or to celebrate the *whole gospel* without the living awareness of the coming again. This is the cause for our hope, for it means the fulfillment of the sovereign purpose of God. Just as the first coming of Jesus Christ can be understood only as the action of God's purpose, so also the second coming. We can no more describe in commonplace detail—as one might describe a tornado, snowfall, invasion by an alien army, or rocket trip to the moon—the coming again than we can describe in commonplace terms the first coming of Jesus Christ in history to all men, or his present coming in conversion to a single person. The language of truth simply is not the language of fact. Yet the *truth* of God's sovereignty requires that his will be done, and at last be done completely and in fact. The coming again means exactly this in Christian faith. As surely as God is sovereign Creator, so is he *sovereign* Redeemer! His work begun in the Christ Incarnate will be completed in the Christ Triumphant. This is the meaning of the coming again. This is why the first Christian confession of faith was a word of confident, expectant hope said in direct address: "Come, Lord Jesus!"

The Oneness of Our Savior with Us

The "whole Christ," then, is not just another particular person who may be described as persons are described. He is *the* particular person who is central in the relationship between God and men. He is the One apart from whom we do not know God. He is the One apart from whom we do not know ourselves. We usually see his personal relationship to God more readily than we see his personal relationship to us. We accept his oneness in being with God, but we have difficulty in accepting his oneness in being with us.

Some husbands and wives know what it means to be one in being with each other. The being, as well as the well-being of each, depends upon the love of the other; and when there is any estrangement, there is a wrongness of the inner being itself. This relationship is other than, and more than, just the expression of loving acts. It is deeper than, and more than, the sum total of the words and acts of love. It is a profound involvement together in a common being. In the marriage service, Christian marriage (holy matrimony) is spoken of as "signifying unto us the mystical union which exists between Christ and his Church." Our relationship to Jesus Christ always is as members of his church, and a relationship that may indeed be called "mystical union." It is vital to Christian life and worship that we know that we have no real being apart from Jesus Christ. "If we live, we live to the Lord, and if we die, we die to the Lord; so then, whether we live or whether we die, we are the Lord's. For to this end Christ died and lived again, that he might be Lord both of the dead and of the living." (Rom. 14:8-9.) In Jesus Christ "it is always Yes. For all the promises of God find their Yes in him. That is why we utter the Amen through him, to the glory of God." (II Cor. 1:19-20.)

This is why incarnation—Jesus Christ become one with us— is inseparable from crucifixion-resurrection, ascension, and coming again. Precisely because he is one with us, and we are made to be one with him, he is our Savior who represents us to God so that,

71

our sins forgiven and our being restored, we may have new life together in him.

We take the time to spell this out because it so often is "watered down" by our thinking of Jesus Christ simply as teacher of great truths and establisher of noble example. When we think of Jesus Christ in this way, we are right back where we started—human beings trying to save ourselves by our own achievements and right living. The fact that we try to live by "Christian principles" rather than by those of some other admirable philosophy does not really change anything. The Old Testament and the writings of various non-Christian religious and moral philosophers present every great *moral* principle that is set forth in Christianity. The crucial difference is in a Savior who redeems us *in being* through personal relationship that reconciles us to God and to one another. What our Savior has done and is doing is the cause, substance, and guide of Christian worship.

To summarize: We depend upon Jesus Christ for the very meaning of ourselves; we depend upon the Holy Spirit for the power to think, will, and respond. Since this is so basic to Christian worship, let us put it yet one further way: We are dependent upon God for life by redemption as well as for life by creation. As John Wesley maintained, there is no such thing as "natural man"; that is, man unaided by the power of God. By *his* power we breathe, think, decide, and love. We are dependent upon him for "raw life"—sheer physical existence. We are dependent upon him for "real life"—the life of human fulfillment. We can no more "save ourselves" into "real life" than we can create ourselves into "raw life."

What then can we do? Nothing alone. But by the power of God—the enabling of the Holy Spirit—we can glorify God and do the good works that God has prepared that we should walk in. (Eph. 2:10c.) The life in Christ to which God calls us is a life of being that includes doing. "For we are his workmanship, created in Christ Jesus for good works." (Eph. 2:10*a, b*.) "Good works" are inseparable from faith; service is inseparable from worship.

The Work of Celebrating the Whole Gospel

We cannot by our own effort *achieve* the benefits of worship, but we can prepare ourselves to receive God's gift of the benefits of worship. By "benefits of worship," we mean "growing up in Christ"—increasing in the knowledge of the meaning of our Lord; becoming more fully given to him in trust; being more dedicated to him in the obedience of good works; receiving the comfort (which is strength as well as peace) of his presence; experiencing forgiveness, renewal, reconciliation, and joy as participants with all Christians in the victory of God in Jesus Christ. However specified, the benefits of worship are expressions of a vital relationship with God in Christ. Just as human friendships that are profound and sustaining are more likely to come to those who are sensitive and responsible in their relationships with other persons, so is our life-giving servanthood to our Lord more likely if we are sensitive and responsible in our relationship to him. "Coming to know the Lord" requires a commitment of mind and a discipline of effort as well as an openness of heart. The General Rules of The Methodist Church enjoin us that we shall continue to evidence our desire for salvation "by doing no harm, by avoiding evil of every kind," and "by attending upon all the ordinances of God." The ordinances are: "The public worship of God. The ministry of the Word, either read or expounded. The Supper of the Lord. Family and private prayer. Searching the Scriptures. Fasting or abstinence." All require a disciplined, alert work—a lively "being fully present" in attention, participation, and receptivity in all the meetings with God that are times of Christian worship.

One essential discipline of work in worship is that of setting ourselves to celebrate the whole gospel of Jesus Christ. "Chance worship" may be moving and enlightening and inspiring in some instances, but in the long pull we do not become mature Christians by responding to Jesus Christ simply as chance interest and occasion may prompt us to do. We need a structured discipline to keep us regularly and fully mindful of the whole meaning of Jesus Christ.

The early Christians knew, from the very beginning of the church, the need for a structured discipline of worship. They met for this purpose on the first day of each week. Sunday worship, then, always has been the basic discipline of corporate worship for Christian people. From the start, Sunday was a weekly celebration of eternal redemption through Jesus Christ. The reality of present redemption was the emphasis rather than a memorial of the resurrection and ascension of the Lord. When we speak of each Sunday as being "a little Easter," we need to have the lively sense of the early Christians that the resurrection which we celebrate is not simply the pivotal aspect of "the gospel given," but is the very reality of our own salvation and present life through Jesus Christ.

With each Sunday being "a little Easter," "big Easter" nevertheless was celebrated once a year. Thus the church began to develop a full discipline to celebrate deliberately the whole gospel of Jesus Christ. This full discipline is called the church year.

The Church Year

All of us are familiar with two major parts of the church year —Christmas and Easter. We look forward each year to hearing again the story of shepherds and angels, of wise men and a star, of a hoped-for Messiah born in a manger. We like to sing about the holy night of adoration around "yon virgin Mother and Child," about a blessed town called Bethlehem, where "the hopes and fears of all the years are met," about our Savior "born a babe and yet a king." Our hearts join the hallelujahs for the Son of God come to be one with us and to redeem us. At Easter, our hearts are exalted as we hear the story of our Lord's being raised from the dead, and when we are again made aware that because he lives we too shall live. And the soaring, rejoicing peace that is not of the world's giving comes to us when we hear that "the trumpet shall sound" to herald the final fulfillment of God's victory, and we are moved by a spirit other than ourselves to live as the resurrected people that we are—by the power of God in Jesus Christ!

In brief, we are accustomed to celebrating Christmastide and Eastertide with the full-feeling, rejoicing thanksgiving that always has characterized Christian worship at its best. We are aware, though, that Christmas and Easter do not comprise all the gospel celebrating that there is to be done, for the gospel story does not consist simply of the birth and the raising from the dead of our Lord—of incarnation and resurrection. The gospel also includes the obedient life of Jesus Christ in deed and word; his revelation as the Savior of all men; his Passion and death; his ascension; his redeeming and eternal kingship. The other five seasons (Advent, Epiphany, Lent, Pentecost, and Kingdomtide) include these emphases. Taking all seven seasons together, we regularly are reminded that the whole of the gospel is the story of God's purposeful love acting in and through Jesus Christ to redeem his whole creation to the fullness of life that is joyful obedience to him.

The church year, then, is an annual plan of worship which is based on the great themes of the gospel of Jesus Christ. The plan is structured on the saving work of Jesus Christ and the Holy Spirit. One aspect of the church year is the list of scripture readings for corporate worship on each Sunday of the year. Such a list is called a lectionary. This list includes a lesson, or lection, from Old Testament, epistle, and Gospel for each Sunday, arranged in keeping with the emphasis of the particular season of the church year. These lessons may be set up on either a one- or two-year plan so that a substantial number of the great passages of Scripture throughout the Bible will be read in meaningful sequence. The sermon usually will be based on one or more of the lessons for a particular Sunday. The Psalms or other responsive readings are designated according to their appropriateness for the various seasons. Hymns and anthems that are especially suited to a season may be selected, though many hymns and anthems rightly may be used in two or more different seasons. Also, one or more of the prayers in a service often catch up the prevailing seasonal theme. In addition to all these verbal acts of worship, many churches have pulpit, lectern, and altar hangings in colors that are associated with the different seasons so as to provide visual reminders of the great gospel themes as they are celebrated. Colors often used in Methodism are: purple for Advent and Lent; white for Christmastide and Eastertide; green for Epiphany and Kingdomtide, and red for Pentecost. So it is that in depth and extent in the services of worship, the whole central gospel is brought to bear upon us as we make the annual round of the church year, which also is called "the Christian year," and may as rightly be called "the gospel year."

The Use of the Church Year

Perhaps we should take time here to say that a rigid following of the church year is not mandatory in The Methodist Church. Neither is the church year the only motif under which the whole gospel of Jesus Christ might conceivably be celebrated. It is God whom we worship, and not a structure or procedure. If the structure or procedure can help us have evangelical (whole gospel) worship, then fine! Let us use such help gladly and devoutly, being free to make whatever well-advised changes may be necessary in particular situations.

With "whole-gospel" worship being our interest, the church year as a structure for worship recommends itself for serious consideration by every Methodist church for several reasons:

it strongly encourages "whole-gospel," scriptural preaching;

it provides for great major lessons from the Holy Scriptures to be read Sunday after Sunday;

It causes us to broaden the scope of our prayers, hymns, and anthem;

it affords a basic "at-homeness" wherever one may be attending a service of worship, which is of importance in any church, but especially so in one which has an itinerant ministry.

The Methodist Calendar of the Seasons of the Church Year

Season	Duration
Advent	Beginning with Sunday nearest November 30 Four Sundays
Christmastide	Beginning with December 25 One to two Sundays
Epiphany	Beginning with January 6 Four to nine Sundays
Lent	Beginning with Ash Wednesday (forty-sixth day before Easter) and going through Easter Even. Six Sundays

77

Eastertide	Beginning with Easter
	Seven Sundays
Pentecost	Beginning with seventh Sunday (fiftieth day) after Easter
	Twelve to seventeen Sundays
Kingdomtide	Beginning with last Sunday in August
	Thirteen to fourteen Sundays

The Shape of the Church Year

The church year, according to present Methodist usage, may best be seen as two great seasons of dual and triple celebration of the gospel of Jesus Christ, each season of celebration being preceded by one of preparation.

Preparation	Celebration
Advent	Christmastide-Epiphany
Lent	Eastertide-Pentecost-Kingdomtide

The Event and Role Emphases of the Seasons of the Church Year

Each season is based on an event or events pertaining to our Lord, and is characterized by one or more of his roles as Savior.

Season	Event	Role
Advent	Second and first comings	Jesus Christ, Judge and anticipated Messiah
Christmastide	Birth	Jesus Christ, God Incarnate
Epiphany	Manifestation to the Wise Men	Jesus Christ, Revealer of God to all men
Lent	Our Lord's forty days in wilderness	Jesus Christ, Revealer of men to themselves
Eastertide	The Resurrection	Jesus Christ, risen Savior

78

Pentecost	The Holy Spirit at first Pentecost	God the Holy Spirit, futhering the work of God the Son
Kingdomtide	Ascension; coming again	Jesus Christ, King eternal

Central Emphases of the Seasons of the Church Year

Advent

Advent is the season for preparing ourselves to celebrate Christmastide and Epiphany. To celebrate as Christians is to enter into the meaning of God's action so that we are renewed in understanding and spirit as his children through the redeeming work of Jesus Christ. Therefore, we do not celebrate carelessly, and so make the gospel ineffectual in our lives. We anticipate with seriousness and hopefulness the representing to us of God's victorious gospel in the seasons of celebration.

Advent prepares us for the high meaning of Christmas and Epiphany as a celebration of the birth of our Lord and his revelation to all men, by reminding us that the Babe of Bethlehem is the risen and ascended Lord "who will come again to judge both the quick and the dead." Therefore, a major emphasis of Advent is Jesus Christ as Judge. Just as there is a profound sense of his judging and condemning our wrongbeing and wrongdoing, so is there awareness of the great hope that it is *Jesus Christ* who is our judge—the One who himself suffered death by the wrongful judgment of men in such a way that *his* judgment of us is not at last condemnation but redemption. This is why we come upon what at first seems strange to us—that the first Sunday of Advent gives attention to the coming again of Jesus Christ. But the right and sure way to prepare for the celebration of the first coming is to bring ourselves before the awesome meaning of the *second* coming. When this is done, Christmas can never be trivial or sentimental, for it means that in Jesus' birth "God has indeed visited and redeemed his people."

The dual emphasis of Christmas and Epiphany being the coming of Jesus Christ by incarnate birth to be the Savior of all men, Advent stresses in four successive Sundays four major ways of the proclaiming of his coming—in the coming again, in the Bible, in the prophets, and by John the Baptist.

George M. Gibson quotes Dom Cabrol:

It is the near approach of the Son of God in the flesh for which one must prepare oneself with greater watchfulness, and by the practice of works of charity; it is the voice of the prophets announcing the Messiah who comes; it is the world awaiting its Redeemer, sighing as the parched ground for the dew of heaven; it is St. Paul exhorting the faithful, awakening them from their sleep upon the vigil of the Coming of Christ; it is John the Baptist, the last of the long line of prophets, who cries from the wilderness, "Prepare ye the way of the Lord!" [2]

Christmastide

Christmastide is the celebration of the Incarnation of Jesus Christ—the birth of the divine Son of God as a full participant in human nature. This is the central emphasis of Christmastide.

The gospel being whole, no one part can be said to be important, as if to imply some other parts are not important. The Resurrection has no meaning apart from the Crucifixion, and is incomplete without the Ascension. So also the Resurrection depends upon the incarnate birth. *Who* was raised up from the dead? God the Son, who was perfectly man, was raised up from

[2] *The Story of the Christian Year* (Nashville: Abingdon Press, 1945), p. 96.

the dead. God's love in the person of his Son, our representative in the person of the only perfect man—this is the One who is God's mystery (Col. 2:2) and our Savior. The Incarnation is the basic mystery of the Christian faith. Jesus Christ's at-once involvement in divine being and in human being is the reason why "the hopes and fears of all the years" were met in Bethlehem on the night of his birth and why the news of his birth is "good news of a great joy which will come to all people."

Epiphany

Epiphany is the season of celebration of the universal revelation of Jesus Christ—of his being "shown forth," "manifested," "epiphanized" as the Savior of all men. Traditionally observed are his "manifestations" to the Wise Men, in his baptism, and in "the first miracle which he wrought in Cana of Galilee."

The emphasis of Epiphany is redemptive revelation. Consequently, it is the season of especial attention to the church as *mission,* so that the missionary work of the church is seen as a continuation of the revelation of our Lord as Savior of all men. It also is well for the season of Epiphany to be a time when the church deals seriously with problems of reason and faith—the relevance of the revealed gospel to people of today whose thought time and thought forms are so very different from those in which the gospel was first set in the midst of men.

Lent

Lent is the season of preparation for the celebration of Eastertide, Pentecost, and Kingdomtide.

In a season of preparation we are concerned with two things: that which we are preparing to celebrate, and our own readiness rightly to celebrate it. During Lent we look at ourselves and the changes of heart and mind that are needed in order for us to celebrate Easter, Pentecost, and Kingdomtide most fully and most

81

meaningfully. We do this by looking ahead especially to Easter and Pentecost—to crucifixion, resurrection, ascension, and the coming of the Holy Spirit; by renewing our awareness of the whole-gospel setting of all that we will celebrate; by giving direct attention to the events; and by engaging in especial self-imposed disciplines of self-denial and service. The self-examination and the penitential self-discipline of Lent are not to make us worthy of celebrating Easter and Pentecost in the sense of becoming entitled to do so because we are good enough, but rather to make us worthy in the sense of being aware, receptive, and eager to participate in the celebration. Though we indeed gain many benefits from our taking part in the celebration, we cannot aim at the benefits that we hope to get and thereby truly prepare ourselves for the celebration. Instead, we look toward the event-cause and the person-cause of our celebration—to the victory through Jesus Christ caused by God. One of the most familiar of the collects exhibits the proper direction of Lenten concern: that we may be made ready for the sole business of loving and worshiping God.

Almighty God, unto whom all hearts are open, all desires known, and from whom no secrets are hid; cleanse the thoughts of our hearts by the inspiration of thy Holy Spirit, that we may perfectly love thee, and worthily magnify thy holy Name; through Jesus Christ our Lord. Amen.

In a season of preparation we must be aware of what we are preparing to celebrate, for this is our goal and inspiration for preparation. We must not, however, let this awareness lead us into premature celebration. Perhaps there is a greater danger of this in Advent than in Lent. In Advent we often begin singing Christmas hymns, and so run ahead of the celebration that is to come in due time. We also thereby cause the preparation to be inadequate. In Lent, Good Friday stands starkly between us and

Easter, and we really cannot bring ourselves to sing, "Christ the Lord is risen today!" three weeks before Easter.

From our human side of things, the central question of Lent is: "Who am I in relationship to Jesus Christ?" From the side of Jesus Christ, Lent is the season of our Lord's revelation of men to themselves. As we attend to the temptations of Jesus, to his deeds and his preaching, to his passion and death, we know two things: one is that we cannot just "be like him" by our own efforts; the other is that we are so identified with him that we cannot know ourselves apart from him. This dual awareness of our inability to save ourselves and of our involvement-in-being with Jesus Christ makes us ready for celebrating most gratefully and joyfully the resurrection of our Lord by which is effected our own new life.

Lent, then, is never a season of penitence for penitence's sake. Lent is in order to Easter and Pentecost just as conviction of sin is in order to redemption.

Passion Sunday and Holy Week

Passion Sunday and Holy Week come at the end of Lent. Passion Sunday is the second Sunday before Easter, and Holy Week begins with Palm Sunday, which is the Sunday before Easter. The other chief days of Holy Week are Maundy Thursday and Good Friday.

Passion Sunday centers upon the suffering of Jesus Christ on our behalf—the purposeful self-giving of our Lord. Passion Sunday bespeaks the humanity of Jesus Christ in his sacrifices for us, for in this he carried in himself the suffering for all sin and all wrong of all time that through him we might be forgiven and caused to live. When we say the Prayer of Consecration in the service of Holy Communion, "in remembrance of his passion," we are being aware that Jesus Christ represented us all in his suffering of concern (Matt. 23:37), his suffering in the Gethsemane prayer (Luke 22:44), his suffering at the scourging (Luke 23:11), and his suffering on the cross.

Palm Sunday marks Christ's kingly authority in the name of the Father. In humble dignity he rode into Jerusalem to lay claim to the single obedience of men to God. In so doing, he opposed the authority of this world and made inevitable either obedience or rebellion. If rebellion, then his death was certain to ensue. However, knowing Palm Sunday as we do from the afterside of the Resurrection and Ascension, and the promise of his coming again, we see it also as an earnest of Christ's heavenly kingship at last to be fulfilled also on earth. Hence, the triumphal entry into Jerusalem catches up all the comings of the Lord—his first coming, his second coming, and his present coming to those of his church. "Blessed be he who comes in the name of the Lord!" (Mark 11:9.)

Maundy Thursday ("Command Thursday," recalling our Lord's command, "Do this in remembrance of me") is the observance of the Last Supper. (Since a chapter will be devoted to baptism and Holy Communion, detailed comment is omitted here.)

Good Friday ("God's Friday") was man's Bad Friday of the Crucifixion which was turned into God's Friday by the Resurrection. Good Friday is the observance of the Crucifixion. The hard reality of the Crucifixion is not to be dismissed or minimized by our casting a premature eye toward the Resurrection as if to say, "But it all turned out all right, so let us not take this too seriously." Indeed, it all did turn out victoriously for God in principle, and so by his grace for us, but the real and serious cost to God and to man is not to be belittled, either in the winning of the crucial battle at the time of the crucifixion-resurrection, or in the time since, when the deadly skirmishes of the "mopping up" have continued. The crucial battle for redemption has been won, but the victory will not have been claimed in full until every creature of God has entered into the new life of reconciliation in Christ. It is altogether sound and right that Good Friday should be observed in deliberate solemnity, with a vigil of meditation and prayer in which each word of Jesus from the cross is duly noted.

It also should be said that services are held in some churches each day of Holy Week, though we have mentioned here only the major and most widely observed services.

Eastertide

Eastertide is a fifty-day season of celebration centering around the Resurrection and the Ascension. Beginning on Easter morning, it continues a sustained emphasis upon the meaning of God's triumph through Jesus Christ.

Just as "raised up" does not mean much unless we know *from what* our Lord was "raised up" (which is to say that the Resurrection has meaning only in relationship to the Crucifixion), so does "raised up from" lack full meaning unless we know *to what* our Lord was raised up. Jesus Christ was not simply raised up from death to life; he was raised up at last to sit at the right hand of the Father. This was the Ascension, occurring forty days after Easter. From the death of the martyred Incarnate Son, he was raised up to be the eternal life of King of kings and Lord of lords —to be the One at whose name "every knee should bow, in heaven and on earth and under the earth, and every tongue confess that Jesus Christ is Lord, to the glory of God the Father" (Phil. 2:10-11.)

Easter Day is the festival of the Resurrection of Jesus Christ, and Eastertide is the season of the meaning of the Resurrection to the church. Our approach to Easter properly is not as a sort of crescendo from which we fall straightway into exhausted flatness. To put it differently, it is a confident and hopeful moving strongly

85

upward from the valley of Lent to a high plateau which stretches from Easter Sunday across the three expanses of Eastertide, Pentecost, and Kingdomtide. Easter, then, is not an isolated pinnacle, but is the high end of a very long mesa on which two other elevations are seen down the way—Pentecost Day and the Festival of Christ the King. From Easter Sunday our worship moves from strength to strength. There is no reason for feeling that the celebration of Easter Sunday has exhausted the resurrection theme, for the very subjunctive of all Christian living is, "If then you have been raised with Christ" (Col. 3:1). Eastertide is the time to appropriate with thankful rejoicing what it means to be "raised up with Christ."

Pentecost

Pentecost is the season of the Holy Spirit as "the Lord and Giver of life" Counselor, and Comforter to the church. While Pentecost is observed as the birthday of the church, we always should be mindful that the church was born and continues in life by the power of the Holy Spirit. (Acts 2.) Therefore, there is much to be said for all our worship in Pentecost being in especial mindfulness of the Holy Spirit, however much our attention may be given to the church during this season.

In the Nicene Creed there is reference to the Holy Spirit as proceeding from the Father and the Son. Whatever else, this way of putting it keeps us aware that what the Holy Spirit does always is at one with the work of Jesus Christ. Our Lord speaks of the Comforter and Counselor being sent by the Father in his name (John 14:26), and encourages his disciples as if to say that the presence of the Counselor is the same as his own continuing Presence (John 16:7). Also, it is the Holy Spirit who will witness to Jesus Christ in the hearts of men, and who is the one by whom we are enabled to say, "Jesus Christ is Lord." (I Cor. 12:33.)

Kingdomtide

Kingdomtide is the latest of the seasons to develop, having begun to be observed by some of the churches in America before 1940. It is possible that The Methodist Church is the only sizable denomination that now follows the practice of having a Pentecost season of twelve to seventeen Sundays and Kingdomtide of thirteen to fourteen Sundays. While there is something to be said for maintaining practices that are reasonably at one with sister churches, it seems clear that the Methodist practice is preferable to a long Trinitytide of twenty-three to twenty-nine Sundays, which season has such comparatively poor grounding for existence at all. Among other things, the long Trinity season leads to the contrived explanation of the church year as having to do with the life and work of Jesus Christ during the first half of the year, and with the response of the Church during the latter half of the year. This is not a very inspired conception of the way that the gospel relates to the church. A substantial Pentecost season that gives due attention to the Holy Spirit and the church, and a substantial Kingdomtide that gives due attention to the eternal and present kingship of Jesus Christ, with the attendant obedient stewardship of his people, provide a much stronger "carry-through" of celebrating the whole gospel of Jesus Christ. It well may be that The Methodist Church may finally mediate between the churches that have a long Pentecost season with a Trinity Sunday, and the churches which have a long Trinity season with a Pentecost Sunday.

Kingdomtide stands solidly in the midst of our daily responsibilities. It says to us that all we do in our personal, social, economic, political, and religious life is under the rulership of Jesus Christ, our eternal King. There is nothing that is not under his governance. Therefore, Kingdomtide has the dual emphasis of the kingship of Jesus Christ and the subjecthood of his followers.

87

Kingdomtide looks upward with the Ascension in awareness of the eternal kingship of Jesus Christ, and looks ahead to the coming again in awareness that the redeeming Savior who is our eternal King also is our ultimate judge. So it is that Kingdomtide has its "event basis" in the Ascension which also relates closely to Easter, and to the coming again which also relates closely to Advent. This is well, for it thereby provides the reminder that the kingship is a "whole-gospel" kingship that is implicit in the celebration throughout the whole of the church year.

Kingdomtide needs to be kept personal. That is, we need to remember that it is the kingship of Jesus Christ that is definitive for the season. In this way we may avoid thinking of the Kingdom as an enterprise that we may undertake to build for God. The "good works, which God prepared . . . that we should walk in them" (Eph. 2:10) are much to the point here. The New Testament constantly exhorts us to the deeds of personal and social responsibility that are the fruits of faith. But what we do, we do in joyful obedience to God and by the enabling of the Holy Spirit; we do in glad and solemn awareness of who is the King that we serve as willing subjects.

By the whole gospel of Jesus Christ, God says his love to us. In whatever way we may find to do it, the celebration of the whole gospel with him seems clearly a right way for us to say our love to God, and "worthily magnify his holy Name."

Chapter 4

PLANNING THE ORDER OF WORSHIP

Let us suppose that a local church has carefully appointed a Commission on Worship to study the worship of the congregation. The order of worship for the main worship service of the week is to be the first major matter with which they concern themselves. Many personal opinions probably would be expressed about one part of the service or another—one may prefer a particular creed, one may think the creed unnecessary; someone would propose that the offering ought to come after the sermon; another would mail a check to the treasurer and eliminate the offering entirely. It soon would become apparent that time for study is necessary and that a basis for discussion needs to be found.

It is the purpose of this chapter to suggest some specific basis on which such discussions may take place. Such studies are expected in The Methodist Church, for Article XXII in the Articles of Religion deals directly with the "rites and ceremonies of churches." (Interestingly enough, this article was taken almost verbatim by Mr. Wesley from the Articles of Religion of the Church of England.)

It is not necessary that rites and ceremonies should in all places be the same, or exactly alike; for they have been always different, and may be changed according to the diversity of countries, times, and men's manners, so that nothing be ordained against God's Word. Whosoever, through his private judgment, willingly and purposely doth openly break the rites and ceremonies of the church to which he belongeth, which are not repugnant to the Word of God, and are ordained and approved by common authority, ought to be rebuked openly (that others may fear to do the like), as one that offendeth against the common order of the church, and woundeth the consciences of weak brethren.

Every particular church may ordain, change, or abolish rites and ceremonies, so that all things may be done to edification.

Here is the mandate to Methodists for the study and understanding of their worship. "Every particular church" probably was not intended to mean each local congregation, but each regional or cultural division; but the obligations upon each local church are large. It is clear that the forms of worship are dynamic and change from culture to culture and from time to time, and they are not to be followed blindly. It is equally clear that the forms of worship are not to be determined by the whims of individuals or small, unofficial groups. The Commission on Worship can find a basis for its work by following the purpose of the Article on Rites and Ceremonies as it looks to both "God's Word" and the "common order of the church" in order "that all things may be done to edification." The suggestions which follow may be of help to this end.

The Norms of the Service

The Theological Norm

The whole service as well as each component part properly is judged first of all by the gospel. A few of the questions to be asked are: Can this be done "in the Name of Jesus Christ our Lord?" Is this in keeping with our best understanding of the biblical message? Does it reveal the nature of man and God as understood by the central insights of the church? Such questions are of the first rank. A failure to conform to the theological norm would eliminate any part of the service.

The Ecclesiastical Norm

Of second rank is the norm which tests a worship service by the usage and practice of the church. Some of the testing questions are: How does our worship compare with the long experience of the church? Is what we are planning considerate of our Methodist tradition in both its Anglican and Free Church background? How does this affirm our place in the whole church of Jesus Christ?

The Psychological Norm

This category is third in importance. The tests under this norm may be suggested by these questions: How do the people in this church understand and talk about the Christian faith? What words, signs, and symbols do they understand best? What are the major cultural patterns of the group? What are the sociological and aesthetic influences of the community?

If there is agreement within the Commission on these three norms, many conflicting ideas may be reconciled. Even within these areas, there are, of course, variations as to particulars, so the planning of worship requires the give-and-take of open minds committed to the gospel.

Vehicles for Worship

The words, acts, and other symbols which have been the normal vehicles for expressing worship are the means that are used in constructing a service. Two broad categories may be considered: those which show forth the acts of God in the drama of redemption; and those which are expressive of man's response to God. These often are so interrelated as to be incapable of sharp divisions, yet both should be recognized. The following materials of worship are widely used throughout the church.

The Bible

From our Old Covenant heritage through the New Covenant, the Bible has been a means both for showing forth God's Word, and for providing a vehicle through which men respond. It is the definitive book of the history of redemption, the incomparable record of the relationship between God and men. The words of the Bible permeate every aspect of the church's worship. The Bible is a major means for the celebration of the gospel by the whole church. List the Bible sources in any service. From the call to worship to the benediction, the language of worship is biblical. Its verbal influence is predominant, its theological influence is central.

Prayer

Prayer is of such importance that some churches designate the whole service as a prayer service. This central conviction that God and men can communicate through prayer determines much of the shape of the service. Prayer always is directed to God, and the prayers serve as one of the chief means of keeping clearly before the worshipers the fact that God is the only object of worship. Each attitude of worship can be expressed prayerfully, and a full service of Christian celebration provides prayerful expressions of these attitudes. The Lord's Prayer, other prayers in the Bible, the vast literature of prayers of the church, and prayers composed for particular times and places become means of centering our thoughts on God in all his attributes and men in all their conditions. The very expression of our deepest thought in prayer helps to clarify the thoughts themselves.

Prayer has a variety of attitudes, such as praise, penitence, petition, intercession, thanksgiving, and dedication; and there are different forms of prayer, such as collects, litanies, bidding prayers, and pastoral prayers.

Creeds

The earliest creeds on record were used in worship. Among the first were baptismal formulas such as the one found in the account of Philip and the Ethiopian eunuch. It is quite possible that Phil. 2:5-11 may have been used as a creed in the early church. In addition to their use in worship, the creeds were used as a teaching device to give to the person preparing to join the church a concise statement of the faith. In addition to their use with the new believer, they also were used to identify and send away the heretic and the enemy of the church.

The creeds of the church have been used in most services of worship from the earliest days, and they continue to be means of response to God as well as proclamation of his word.

Music and Hymns

Music has been a part of man's worship in every culture—from the most primitive to the most civilized. References to music in the Bible and throughout the history of the church show its important place in Christian worship. Those of us who are heirs of the Reformation and the Wesleyan revival are particularly blessed with a heritage of music as a vehicle of worship.

Instrumental music expresses thoughts and feelings which can be expressed in no other way, though it is not capable of the sharp definitions which can be made with words. Some groups of Christians have limited instrumental music; others have eliminated it altogether. However, the mainstreams of church tradition have used musical instruments to express praise, penitence, thanksgiving, dedication, and other feelings to God and to call forth from the people these feelings. The power of music to inspire many reactions, some quite foreign to worship, calls for diligent care to insure the best possible use of this means of expression.

The hymn is a wedding of music and words which affords the church one of its most vital elements of worship. The psalms set to music, especially under Calvin, gave another name to the service—church praise. Hymns became a principal means of the celebration of the gospel, and they still hold a major place. The psalms first, then other passages of scripture, and poems of praise set to the music of various cultures went hand in hand with prayer as central acts of worship. In more recent years, poems of teaching, encouragement, and exhortation which are directed toward men instead of God have been set to music and have become the basis of what often are called gospel songs.

Those who plan the service of worship are under obligation to make a judgment as to both words and music; and there are many factors which sometimes clash. The words of the hymn or anthem are especially influential because they are most readily understood by the majority of the people. It is of great value to the congregation to have the words of the anthem printed in the bulletin so that the verbal message of the anthem may readily be available. Singing untrue words to fine music should be unthinkable. By the same token, singing true words to unsuitable music should not be done. Defining suitable or unsuitable music is not easy, but the norms of worship can be of help in doing it. The congregation is fortunate which has musicians who can make their art an offering to God and an effective means for the whole church to celebrate the gospel.

Sermon

The Protestant Reformation reinstituted the importance of preaching in Christian worship. Luther, Zwingli and Calvin saw the worship of the church as a proclamation of the Word. All valid means of worship aid in this proclamation of Jesus Christ, God's Word. But, they insisted, this Word may be perverted if there is not the proclamation through preaching. Luther was as disturbed over the sermon becoming a "word" from the mind of the preacher as over the elimination of the sermon from the Mass. The sermon to Luther was the contemporary and relevant proclamation of the scriptures appointed for the day. He even suggested in the German Mass and Order of Service in 1526 that perhaps sermons should be prepared to be read by the preachers "for the sake of the preachers who could not do any better, but also to prevent the rise of enthusiasts and sects." [1]

The church has never considered the preaching of the sermon to be a sacrament, but the sermon does hold a central place as a means of showing forth the Word. The Word, which is another New Testament name for God, constitutes the validity of all worship, and the sermon is considered to be a chief means for its proclamation. It is of no small significance that the Vatican Council, meeting in the fall of 1963, studied the important place of preaching in the Mass—over four hundred years after Luther!

John Wesley faced a somewhat similar situation in eighteenth-century England, where preaching had been virtually eclipsed in

[1] Quoted from Bard Thompson, *Liturgies of the Western Church* (New York: The World Publishing Company, 1961), p. 132.

the worship of the Established Church. To Wesley the call to preach was not the same thing as the call to be a minister. The Wesleyan revival, therefore, moved forward with a preaching emphasis unmatched in church history.

The sermon is a vital part of Christian worship as a central means of proclamation, teaching, and exhortation to the church. Through the words of the preacher the Word of God may be made explicit. The preacher's freedom comes under the yoke of the biblical message. The sermon may not necessarily be an exposition of the particular scripture lesson for the day, but it ought always to be an exposition of God's Word. The preacher is a "herald of the King" who acts only as a messenger.

The sermon is also a translation of this message into the language of the people. The sermon is that part of the worship of the church that is relevant at the moment and in the locale in which it is preached. The great sermons which have been preserved in the Bible and in the church are great in part because they were so clearly true at the time they were spoken.

The sermon which is oriented both to the biblical message and man's current condition becomes an illumination to the whole of the church's worship, as well as to the scattered church's obedience in the world. This awesome dual responsibility is dramatically set forth when the bishop ordains an elder in The Methodist Church. The candidate kneels and puts his hand on the Bible while the bishop says on behalf of the church: "Take thou authority as an elder in the Church to preach the Word of God, and to administer the holy Sacraments in the congregation."

There is one other dimension of the sermon which must be considered if the liturgical principles of Christian worship are to be properly observed. This is the dimension of hearing. Both Luther and Calvin were concerned with the "inner word" of preaching.

This is more than just that which is heard and comprehended, it is what the Holy Spirit makes known to the hearer. Listening to the sermon requires more than quiet attention; it requires open expectancy and active participation in the proclamation. A sermon is not complete until it is heard in faith and used as the Bread of Life, and this is the act of God the Holy Spirit in both preacher and hearer.

Acts of Worship

We *do* as well as say or sing our worship. Most Christians stand for praise, kneel or bow for prayer, and sit or stand to listen. Many churches have acts of reverence, such as making the sign of the cross or genuflecting upon entering or leaving the church. Methodism includes those who represent a wide variety of practices. Our *Book of Worship* makes few suggestions or demands at this point.

"Going to the altar" in Methodism has meant going to the kneeling rail. There the Holy Communion is administered to the kneeling congregation, babies are brought there for baptism, couples go there for their wedding vows and kneel to receive the church's blessing, penitent sinners have been called to kneel there, and vows of church membership are taken there, prayers of rededication are prayed there, and the bodies of our loved ones are taken there at the funeral. "Going to the altar" is one of the chief acts of Methodist worship.

The offertory movement is another dramatic act. Placing money in the offering plate, taking the plates to the table and dedicating them there as the congregation stands and sings and prays is doing something that can never be fully expressed by words alone.

Processionals are an active symbol of the gathering church, and recessionals symbolize the church scattering into the world. The

97

lighting of candles may be a sign of the Light of the World in whose name we gather for worship, and extinguishing the candles may be a sign of the end of the service. Each movement by the minister and the congregation communicates something, and each act provides opportunity for valid participation in the celebration of the gospel.

Directions

Closely associated with both words and acts are the directions given the congregation by the minister. These need not be elaborate, and churches which use bulletins may not need any verbal directions to call the people to each part of the service. The ease with which the worshipers move from praise to prayer to hearing or to other movements in the service is dependent on the dignity, the clarity, and simplicity of the directions. These are neither military commands nor timid suggestions, but they are the directions which move the service decisively and with certainty. The calls to prayer and praise by versicles, and the calls to listen to scripture and sermon by ascriptions and graduals, are effective in leading the people to worship together.

Buildings and Furnishings

The meaning of the building and furnishings of the church is discussed in a later chapter.

Summary

These symbols and tools which are available to the church in celebrating the gospel may be distorted to become ends in themselves. When this happens it is idolatry. The prophets who spoke God's word of condemnation of the feasts and solemn assemblies (see Amos 5:21-24) knew how subtle the temptation to substitute forms for authentic response. The choice we face, however, does not lie in whether we use tools of worship or not; but rather in whether or not the materials we use for worship are clear means that show forth and celebrate the gospel.

Patterns of Worship

A study of orders of worship from different traditions will show diverse forms but an underlying similarity of content and movement. A logic lies at the foundation of every well-ordered Christian service that conforms to the general pattern of the story of redemption. One might work on the assumption that any celebration of the gospel by the church which proclaims the gospel and gives the worshipers an opportunity for a full response is a "good" service. Given the fullness of the Christian message and the means for proclamation and celebration, the church must determine a pattern and rationale for the service which meets the norms set forth at the beginning of this chapter.

The Eucharistic Pattern

The order of service which probably has the most ancient background is that which combined the services of the synagogue with the service of the upper room. (The upper room service, as recorded by John, generally refers to the meals of the apostles when the risen Christ appeared. It also means the service on the night before the crucifixion recorded in the other gospels and in Corinthians.) The first part of the service, which is sometimes called antecommunion, was a service for the believers as well as those in training (catechumens). There was included in this portion of the service hymns, creeds, scripture readings, psalms, and prayers. Following this part of the service the nonmembers withdrew and the Communion service began. This started with the offering of bread and wine, continued with the prayers of preparation and consecration, and concluded with the other actions of the sacrament.

This pattern is followed by most of the Communion rituals

used today. In the Free Church tradition, if the Holy Communion is not celebrated, the sermon stands in the stead of the sacrament, rather than being a commentary on the lections—as in the synagogue pattern. This may account for the money offering coming before the sermon in most Methodist churches, as well as in Free Church denominations.

The Morning Prayer Pattern

Though the Holy Communion has been the normative service in Christendom, the monastic orders developed what became known as choir offices at seven intervals during each day and night. The English services of common prayer for morning and evening were, in large measure, an adaptation of this monastic practice to the parish church. This service, which became the pattern for daily worship in the Church of England, has had a profound effect upon the worship of the churches in the entire English-speaking world. A revision of this order of common prayer was made by Mr. Wesley and sent to American Methodists. It was honored more in the breach than in practice, yet its form was not wholly abandoned.

The service of morning prayer in the Book of Common Prayer followed this pattern: scripture sentences, call to confession, the general confession, the absolution or remission of sins, the Lord's Prayer, the call to praise, praise by canticle and psalm, and the *Gloria Patri,* the first scripture reading appointed, another canticle of praise, the second appointed scripture lesson, a canticle of praise, the Apostles' or Nicene Creed; and then there may be a sermon, though it is not required, and the closing prayers—a collect for the day and prayers of general intercession and thanksgiving, the closing grace or benediction. One of the striking features of this service was its congregational participation. It was written in the language of the people and the book was in the hands of the worshipers and read by the people together—common worship.

Both its theology and its language have been of profound influence for over four centuries.

The Isaiah Pattern

The sixth chapter of Isaiah is a record neither of Christian nor of congregational worship, yet it does present in one logical order the focus of worship upon God, the recognition of creatureliness by man as sinner, the forgiveness of sin, the call of God, the response in thanksgiving and the offering of self, and the assurance of God's blessing and guidance. This is often used in planning Christian worship services, chiefly for its step-by-step presentation of God's action and man's response. It lends itself for adaptation to either of the patterns discussed above as well as others, even though it does not contain the essential *content* of Christian worship.

The Service: General Characteristics

The intention of this study is not to present a particular order of worship, yet all the essential meaning of Christian worship must finally be expressed in some particular order. The following analysis is made in terms of The Methodist Church with its variety of worship forms. The service we have in mind is the principal service of worship which the largest number of members attend, usually on Sunday morning. In most Methodist churches this does not include Holy Communion on the majority of Sundays. Each church follows one of the suggested orders of worship in the *Methodist Hymnal* or the *Book of Worship* that is best suited to its own situation. An understanding of any one of the services includes the following considerations.

Wholeness

We are creatures of time; therefore, the service will need to flow from one emphasis to another. It is important, however, to recog-

101

nize that the parts of the service are only parts of a whole. Indeed, the act of worship itself is only a part of the unity of life which links worship and work. The church which gathers for worship is the same church which scatters for service in the world. Similarly, praise itself has within it the marks of confession. As one meaning of the Christian's response is emphasized, all other aspects are present. The wholeness of the gospel in its proclamation and teaching is present, yet the wholeness cannot be known aside from its specific parts. Each service of worship properly includes the total message as it moves from part to part. No particular teaching of the gospel can stand in isolation.

Rhythm

Each service must move from one emphasis to another proclaiming the gospel and giving the congregation an opportunity to respond appropriately. Common worship is more than a dramatic re-presentation of redemption, but the rules of dramatic production for motion and rhythm do apply. Even the most beautiful tone loses its beauty when it becomes a monotone. A service at its best will have several high points followed by opportunities for contemplation and absorption and preparation for the next high moment.

Liturgy

Liturgy means "the work of the people." Liturgical worship only means that the worship is the service of all the people gathered. Worship is not a "spectator sport" to which people come to see and hear minister and choir perform. All the people praising, praying, hearing, affirming, offering, as members one of another, are answering God's call to the whole church to worship. The more the whole congregation is given an opportunity to participate actively in every response, the more our worship will be the "work of the people" in glorifying God.

The Service: Movements

Recognition

Recognition is a term used to designate that part of the service of worship called adoration and confession. This more inclusive word is used in order to avoid the danger of implying that *we* initiate worship. Recognition, therefore, includes three aspects of this one act.

First there is God's recognition of us. It is the very act of God the Holy Spirit which enables us to gather in the community of faith. The prelude itself is the accompaniment of this Pentecostal affirmation. The call to worship, or introit, is not a call from man to men, but a call from God to men through his minister.

The second aspect of recognition is man's recognition of God. A hymn directed to God in praise and wonder is the proper response to God's call. An invocation also is a proper form of recognition which may precede or follow the opening hymn if desired.

If we properly recognize who God is, we then recognize who we are before God. This is the third part of recognition. We do not think of God in isolation, for to see him as Creator and Redeemer is to see ourselves as creatures and sinners offered redemption in Jesus Christ. This section of the service usually follows the initial recognition of God, although there are many features of this recognition which will be recurring throughout the hour. A prayer of confession of our creatureliness ought to give the whole body of members an opportunity to express the fact of our sin and the reality of our sins. If at all possible the congregation should pray this together by means of some common prayer. They may, however, pray it together by uniting with the pastor as he voices the prayer for the congregation.

103

No prayer of the confession of sin rightly stands alone. Confession ought always to be followed by an assurance of forgiveness. A scripture sentence may assure God's forgiveness, or a declaration of pardon in other than scriptural terms may be used. A prayer for pardon is usually implied in the confession, and still does not express what God has promised; it only petitions God for it. Different rituals have designated this movement as absolution, words of assurance, comfortable words, God's gracious word. No matter what it is called, if the good news of redemption is not proclaimed and received, it can hardly be Christian worship.

In both traditional and contemporary services, this section often includes the Lord's Prayer in which all the people join. Having received the judgment and mercy of God's grace, we unite with the whole church in the prayer taught us by its head.

This recognition that we are sinners forgiven moves again to recognition of God as the giver of this new life; hence, the church stands in praise. Usually a psalm of praise or other suitable canticle or responsive reading is used as an act of praise, and this is followed by the ancient doxology, *Gloria Patri,* either said or sung. It is important to realize that this is not properly a scripture lesson, but an act of praise to God by means of a biblical poem.

The final portion of this movement may be a recognition of who we are by call and by hope as a community. The *Hymnal* and the *Book of Worship* contain several creeds, and the Commission will wish to use norms with care to determine which creed should be used. The position of the creed may be here, though some Methodist services have it immediately following the first hymn, and older traditions place it as a response to the scripture lessons.

If a service of baptism is to occur, it may come at this point to affirm God's grace in calling the church into being and his continued reception of new life into its body.

Proclamation

Many rationales for worship designate a section of the service as the Service of the Word. This has much to commend it when seen from the standpoint of the reading from the Bible and the preaching of the sermon. Yet the term "Word" has so much more meaning in Christianity than this limited use. The Gospel of John has made "Word" synonymous with Jesus the Christ. In this sense all Christian worship is a Service of the Word.

The proclamation movement begins with a reading from the Bible. A planned series of scripture readings in keeping with the doctrines of the church gives to the congregation an opportunity to hear the great passages of the whole Bible. The *Book of Worship* offers a plan of reading (called a lectionary), and other plans are offered in service books of several denominations covering one or two years. Some lectionaries suggest daily readings suitable for use in homes. The revival of biblical theology in our time is having a marked effect upon our worship in the increased reading of the Bible in our services, and in the church school. Readings from both Testaments in keeping with the church year are a powerful proclamation of the gospel to the church.

How much reading will people hear and understand at one sitting? This is a legitimate question which cannot be answered easily. Certainly there ought to be enough of a passage to carry its meaning. It should be read by one who understands the passage and is able to read it so that it may be understood. When two lessons are read, the first should be followed by some response of gratitude and praise. A suitable hymn, canticle, litany, or anthem may be fitting.

Generally the first lesson is from the Old Testament. The second lesson is usually from the New Testament, and follows the response to the first reading. If the Bible is viewed in its unity, the position of a particular lesson is not so important. It is important that the Bible be made available to the church at worship as a proclamation of God's Word. Whether the sermon is related to the particular readings is of secondary importance, for the Bible itself can stand on its own witness.

Response to the Word in the Bible readings may take any of several forms. In the morning prayer pattern the creed is placed here. This is more than intellectual assent to the faith of the church. It is the raising of the standard, the union with the martyrs, the placing of trust without reservation.

The worshipers have been brought now to a height of response which can be completed in prayer. Prayers of praise and gratitude, petition and intercession, remembrance and resolve may be in order. These prayers may be prepared and prayed by the pastor in recognition of the needs of the flock and on behalf of the "whole state of Christ's Church" as well as for the human family. These prayers may be printed in the bulletin or selected in the *Hymnal* and prayed by all the people. The one who prays on behalf of the congregation will need to take care to see that the prayers are easy to understand and follow, limited in time, and directed to God so as to give the congregation the best opportunity to make the prayers their own. This is the practice of the faith that in prayer God and men communicate.

In the majority of the services in our *Book of Worship* a money offering is made as a token of thanksgiving for that which we have received from God. An offering of money in our complex economic society is a fitting symbol of this thanksgiving, as offerings of food were in earlier times. The new life which we receive from God who brings us together, offers us judgment and pardon, reveals himself through his mighty acts recorded in the Bible and made known in Jesus Christ, can demand only the response of our whole lives. The money represents our work and stewardship of all which

God has given. We place this money on the table in thanksgiving and in the trust that, as we offer our lives to him, he can transform "these creatures" into newness of life. This consecration is not a song of gratitude, but a prayer for the miracle of God's power to transform. Here is an act affirming, in part, the meaning of the death and resurrection of Jesus Christ.

The offering made before the sermon ought to be considered as the first offering and a part of the larger oblation which comes at the climax of the service. This follows very closely the eucharistic pattern which has the offering at the beginning of the Communion, then the completion of the movement in the prayer which follows the distribution of the bread and wine.

Following the offering is a suitable time for those who have been trained for church membership to be received. Methodism's rediscovery of its need to train persons in the meaning of membership is reflected in the ways in which the church receives its new members. By calling the candidates to the chancel and giving the vows in the presence of the people in the midst of the service, the congregation reaffirms its membership, receives the new members, and welcomes them. The response for the congregation in the *Hymnal* may be read and thus give each member an opportunity to express an audible welcome.

The movement of proclamation continues in the rhythm of showing forth response and preparation. As a preparation for the sermon, a hymn or suitable anthem may be sung. The sermon itself becomes the solemn act of the church's representative who is ordained to proclaim this timeless word in a clear and timely and relevant way. The sermon becomes a vehicle of God's Word, not only at the pulpit, but also at the pew. The speaking *and* the hearing constitute the climate for proclamation. Those who preach must understand the nature of their function, but it is of equal importance that those who listen understand theirs.

The Commission on Worship has the important responsibility of helping to train the membership in the acts of worship, and this is needed at the point of hearing the sermon too. The sermon is not a performance by a speaker before an audience; it is a translation of a message already given. It is the message from the King delivered by a herald. It is given in the belief that Christ is present where two or three gather in his name and that the stuff of life— bread and wine and water and people—can bear this revelation. Therefore, we listen openly and expectantly, knowing that God may use these words to speak his Word.

Oblation

Most of the orders of worship in Christendom have difficulty finding a proper way to close a service of worship. The Roman Mass actually announces the end of the service some time before the final blessing. What does one say, how does one act to express the offering of oneself to God who has given of himself totally in Jesus Christ? How can so profound a thanksgiving be expressed? How can the relationship of worship and all the rest of life be shown in unmistakable terms?

It might as well be recognized that all words and acts and hymns and offerings are incapable of a full expression of that which is inexpressible. Yet we are called to express this as forcefully as possible.

Following the sermon, there may be a prayer stating to God the people's highest intention to live in terms of the word proclaimed. Our hymnody abounds in great hymns of commitment which offer us the words and music to express our thanksgiving and praise. As suggested earlier, some churches use the offering of money here as one means of expressing this oblation. The "invitation to Christian discipleship" at this point is much more than an invitation to church membership, though it may certainly include this choice to the nonmember. The real invitation is to accept this life which is given, and now live!

With prayers expressed or unexpressed, the church receives the benediction of God pronounced by the minister and turns toward the "world to come." The recessional may symbolize the scattering of the church, when the people move out to live in obedience. The work, the family, the neighbors, the enemies, the needs, are all areas where our real offering is made and where God makes himself known. God meets us in our neighbor's need and in the unexpected events of life, and so we turn again on the next Lord's Day to join the fellow members in recognition, proclamation, and oblation—one life, under God, facing in many directions.

Chapter 5

THE SACRAMENTS

The sacraments are services of worship. As such, they are subject to the same basic principles as any other service of Christian worship. However, the sacraments also are distinctive as sacraments, for they are specific actions which involve the physical elements of water and of bread and wine, and which are related to particular words said and things done by the Lord. To put it a bit differently, Christian sacraments are actions including the use of physical elements that were commanded or recognized by our Lord, according to certain New Testament passages, as means of initiating and nurturing persons as Christians. The Methodist Church recognizes two sacraments:[1] baptism is the initia-

[1] Though The Methodist Church recognizes only two *sacraments,* it may be said that the ordinances of confirmation, ordination, marriage, and burial are taken with that devout seriousness that causes them to be sacramental in tone and effect.

tion sacrament; Holy Communion is the nurturing sacrament.

The two scriptural passages that most frequently are cited as evidence of our Lord's having established baptism and Holy Communion are Matt. 28:19 and I Cor. 11:23-26. The principal basis for the validity of the sacraments, however, is the very nature of the whole of his gospel to which the entire Scriptures and the life of the church attest.

We now need to look in some detail at the meaning of baptism and Holy Communion. Confirmation also must be considered briefly in connection with baptism.

Baptism

Baptism is an action of God through his church. It is an action of God that is specific and personal, an action by which God claims a particular person into his victory through Jesus Christ. "Do you not know that all of us who have been baptized into Christ Jesus were baptized into his death? We were buried therefore with him by baptism into death, so that as Christ was raised from the dead by the glory of the Father, we too might walk in newness of life." (Rom. 6:3-4.)

It is a minister who places water on the head of a person to be baptized and says the words of blessing. It is a congregation of people who proclaim the Christian faith in this act of baptism, and take the responsibility of nurturing the one baptized in the Christian life. These are the human agencies through whom God acts, but the action that is done is no less God's action. Rather, this is the way that God has created his church and has perpetuated the faith from generation to generation.

The mode of baptism that most directly symbolizes union with Jesus Christ in his death and resurrection is immersion. Being put

---

Furthermore, these ordinances depend upon the sacraments of baptism and Holy Communion for their full meaning.

under the water and then being brought up out of the water signifies the going down into death and being raised up into life—dying to the old self and living anew in Christ. (Col. 3:3.) Baptism by sprinkling symbolizes the cleansing from sins and the liberating from the *principle* of sin by the redeeming work of Jesus Christ. This awareness is caught up in the statement in John Wesley's Aldersgate testimony: "And an assurance was given me that he had taken away my sins, even mine, and saved me from the law of sin and death." Baptism by pouring symbolizes the outpouring of the Holy Spirit—the "Lord and Giver of life" in the midst of the people, the Enlightener moving our minds to faith, and enabling us to say that Jesus Christ is Lord, the Comforter sustaining our hearts in hope. Immersion, sprinkling, pouring—dying and rising with Christ, forgiveness, and the gift of the Holy Spirit—all are aspects of the work of Jesus Christ in saving us from death to life. In fact, *each* mode is a way of understanding the *whole* work of Jesus Christ as Savior. Therefore, each mode of baptism participates in the meaning of the other two, so it does not matter which mode is used. Methodism recognizes and uses all three, and no Methodist properly thinks that one mode is better than the others. Convenience is likely to dictate that sprinkling and pouring be used more than immersion. It would be unfortunate, however, for The Methodist Church to lose immersion as a mode of baptism. Even infants were immersed in the early days of Methodism.

When a person of whatever age is baptized by whatever mode "in the name of the Father, and of the Son, and of the Holy Spirit," he is claimed by God as his child of redemption. He thereby is made a member of the living covenant of God in Christ. God has not proposed this covenant; he has established it. This covenant is not a bargain, not a contract, not an agreement, but the very condition for life itself defined and provided by God in Christ, secured by his own free pledge, and laid upon us by his sovereign love. As in all else, it is the purposeful action of God that is crucial. God's claim upon a person in baptism is not a proposal that he commit himself to God as if there were some other livable alternative. Rather, it is a laying hold of the baptized person by the gracious love of God that will not let him go.

The "victorious covenant" is first of all the Covenant Person, Jesus Christ. He is God's Word. His own baptism at the hands of John the Baptist is a part of his own total obedience to God. But the "great baptism"—the one redeeming baptism for all mankind— is his baptism down into death and up into life, his crucifixion and resurrection. Through and in him God has said to us all there is to be said about life and death, and has done the thing that had to be done in order for us to live. The people of the covenant, the members of the covenant community, the sharers in God's victory, are those who are conjoined with the Covenant Person by whom God effects his victory, and so participate in what he has done for us all. This "membership in Christ" is the essential heart of all that it means to be a Christian.

Baptism is the act by which we are joined to Christ. "For by one Spirit we were all baptized into one body. . . . Now you are the body of Christ and individually members of it." (I Cor. 12:13, 27.) The church, consisting of all baptized members, is the body of Christ. And so, we, belonging to Christ, belong to one another, for "the Church is catholic, universal, so are all her actions; all that she does belongs to all. When she baptizes a child, that action concerns me; for that child is thereby connected to that head which is my head too, and ingrafted into that body whereof I am a members." [2]

Infant Baptism Definitive

Infant baptism is definitive of all baptism. This is true because

[2] John Donne, "Devotions upon Emergent Occasions, XVII."

every person, whether seventy years or seven weeks, is an infant in Christ when he is baptized. Every baptized person always is growing up in the meaning of his baptism. For each of us, baptism "ended the way to Christ, and began the life *in* Christ." [3] To grow up in the meaning of baptism is to grow up in Christ.

God's redeeming act in the whole life and work of Christ, and centrally in his death and resurrection, precedes any decision or act on our part. Therefore, baptism is the once-and-for-all reminder of the gracious love of God that precedes any response we may make. So baptism is not to be repeated. The fact that a person, come of age, does not remember the actual event of his baptism as an infant is not ground for repeating the baptism. Rather, one who was baptized as an infant should be taught the meaning of this holy sacrament so that he may know that God has loved him all the while and has personally claimed him as his own child by redemption.

Does this mean, then, that God's love for a child is dependent upon the child's being baptized? Not at all. God loves his every child by creation. When a child is presented at the altar for baptism, it is as if God, through his church, takes the child in his arms, saying, "By this act I mark you, my child of creation, as my child in redemption through my beloved Son." The child is given a Christian name; he is named as God's child in Christ. (This is why some churches refer to infant baptism as "christening.") The child from then on is one whom God has claimed as wholly his own to live his life in joyful dedication to his creating and redeeming Father.

As infant baptism sets the relationship between God and the child, so does it set the relationship between the parents and the child. In the British Methodist service of baptism it is said to the

---

[3] P. T. Forsyth, *The Church and the Sacraments* (Naperville, Ill.: Allenson, 1949), p. 203.

parents: "You are come here to acknowledge that this, your child, belongs to God, to dedicate him to God in holy baptism, and to receive him again as from the hands of God to be trained as a disciple of our Lord and Saviour Jesus Christ." So the child is identified to his own parents as a child of God, and their relationship to their own child is in central responsibility to God.

It should further be said that the whole church, and this congregation in particular, is godparent or sponsor at every baptism. Natural parents, parents who have adopted a child, or sponsor, represent the church in taking the vows to nurture this child in the Christian faith. When an adult is baptized, a member of the church (perhaps a member of the Commission on Membership and Evangelism) may be asked to stand with the person to be baptized as a representative sponsor for the church. The presence of the sponsor undergirds the understanding that every person is baptized as an "infant in Christ," and is in need of growing up in the Christian faith.

Yet another reason for pressing infant baptism as definitive of all baptism is the primal need each of us has for the assurance of ultimate security. For Christians, this can mean only the certainty of God's love. How is this more livingly conveyed to a child than by rearing him in the meaning of baptism as the action of God specifically expressing his unreserved love for him? Our essential security always seems to be at once that which is given to us and that which is claimed from us. A baptized person who understands his baptism is one who knows that he has been given God's love by no deserving on his own part, and who is claimed to live wholly for God because there is no other real life. Martin Luther frequently would say when things were rough and he needed encouragement for his faith, "I was baptized." This is to say that God loves me and always has; that God loves me and always will. It reminds me of who I am and who I am called to be.

There are legitimate questions, however, about insisting that infant baptism is definitive of all baptism. What is the scriptural basis for it? What was the practice of the early church? How can an adult be baptized as if he were an infant? What about other churches that practice only adult baptism?

We should not hesitate to acknowledge that the clearest instances of baptism in the New Testament are those of adult baptism; however, this is not surprising. A new missionary movement such as the New Testament church could gain new members only as converts, and naturally they were adults. It should especially be noted that there is not one instance in the New Testament or in the writings of the early church of an adult's being baptized whose parents were Christians when he was born. In other words, children born to Christians were all baptized as infants or were considered to be members of the covenant community by inheritance.[4] The conclusion to be drawn is that infant baptism was the overwhelming practice in the early church.

What of a person who is not baptized as an infant? How can he receive infant baptism? Obviously he cannot do so by the calendar, but he can do so by spirit and intention. If we are clear that baptism is a God-initiated beginning of life in Christ, then an adult can be baptized as a "babe in Christ." He may say in effect, "I know that I cannot save myself and I throw myself upon the mercy of God. I am as dependent upon him for salvation as a baby is upon parents for food and care. I do not pretend to know all about the Christian faith and life, but I want to know it and to live it." If the adult happens to be a person of inquiring mind who is insistent upon

[4] See such studies as W. F. Flemington, *The New Testament Doctrine of Baptism* (Greenwich, Conn.: The Seabury Press, 1948); Oscar Cullman, *Baptism in the New Testament* (Naperville, Ill.: Allenson, 1958); Joachim Jeremias, *Infant Baptism in the First Four Centuries* (Philadelphia: The Westminster Press, 1961); Donald M. Baillie, *The Theology of the Sacraments* (New York: Charles Scribner's Sons, 1957).

learning all he can about the Christian faith before he is baptized, and he does so, then surely his baptism is clear to him primarily as a gracious act of God rather than primarily a result of his own knowledge and decision. He appropriates by earnest the meaning of an infant baptism in which he has not been reared but wishes that he had. There is, then, only *one* baptism for persons of all ages. It is the baptism that is the act of God through his church to initiate a person into membership in Jesus Christ.

As to the other churches which practice only adult, or "of-age," baptism, let us appreciate their point of view even while preferring ours.[5] Their emphasis is upon definite personal commitment prior to baptism and upon the importance of baptism as an actually remembered personal experience. They also appeal to the Scriptures as explicitly supporting only adult baptism, but this interpretation of the scriptural accounts and of early church practices seems to us to be inadequate. Commitment and "supportive memory," however, are indeed important and living values. Even so, our ground seems clear for maintaining that the Methodist approach to baptism is more fully in accord with the whole meaning of the gospel, to the relationship between God's grace and a person's faith, and to deep human needs other than personal commitment and supportive memory.

Though infant baptism is definitive of all baptism, it is evident that the meaning of baptism in a person's life is not appropriated apart from personal commitment. The service in which one accepts and affirms the meaning of his baptism is confirmation.

Confirmation: An Essential Sequel to Infant Baptism

Confirmation is the action of a baptized person in confirming in the presence of the church the acceptance of his baptism in an act

---

[5] One of the best statements on "believer's baptism" is by Karl Barth, *The Teaching of the Church Regarding Baptism* (Naperville, Ill.: Allenson, 1956).

of personal commitment, and the action of God through his church in confirming and blessing him in his commitment to this baptismal faith.

When a person, regardless of the age at which he was baptized, has been instructed in the meaning of baptism and of the Christian faith, he then is called upon to acknowledge and affirm the faith in which he has been reared and taught. At confirmation a person in effect says: "I give thanks for what was done for me by God and his church that I could not do for myself. I now consciously affirm the meaning of my baptism, and seriously and gratefully take upon myself the duties and privileges of being a member of the church of Jesus Christ." Confirmation, then, is at once a "gathering of the memory" of the faith in which one has been reared and a personal commitment to Jesus Christ as his Savior and Lord.

A person is *confirmed* in the church of Jesus Christ; he is *received into the membership* of The Methodist Church. Baptism and confirmation constitute membership in the universal church of Jesus Christ. For this reason, our confirmation vows center around the meaning of baptism. However, each member of the church of Jesus Christ has a specific church home for worship and work, and a person should be in accord with the emphasis, polity, and program of the particular denomination into which he is received as a member. For this reason, a person takes such a vow of loyalty to The Methodist Church as a part of the universal church when he is received into its membership.

It is important for a person of whatever age to be baptized at one time and to be confirmed and received into membership at another. This is the best way to keep clear the respective meanings of these acts. The normal procedure is for a person to be instructed in the meaning of the Christian faith and life between the time that he is baptized and the time that he is confirmed. The time of instruction may be several years in the instance of a person's being baptized in infancy, or it may be only several months, or even weeks. Even if an adult has been thoroughly instructed prior to his baptism, it may be well to wait at least until the next Sunday before he is confirmed.

This timing of baptism and confirmation keeps us aware of the relationship between God's grace and our faith. God's grace (his loving power moving to effect his holy will) always comes before our response in faith. If we associate baptism primarily with God's grace, we are much more likely to remain aware of the primacy of his will in our lives. Our faith is our personal relationship to God in belief, adoration, and obedience, and our faith is called forth— it is created—by God's grace.

So it is that we are claimed, called, and branded by God through baptism as his child in Christ; we are nurtured in God's love by being reared in his church; in due time we are enabled by God's grace to confirm by personal commitment his claim upon us and to assume our responsibility in joyful obedience to him; and we are blessed and affirmed by God in this confirmation.

The meaning of baptism is recapitulated in confirmation in a new dimension of conscious commitment. The meaning of both baptism and confirmation is increased throughout our lives as we "go on to maturity" in Christ. (Heb. 6:1.) Among the most important means of maturing as Christians that God has provided for us is the Holy Communion. Whereas baptism and confirmation are a once-and-for-all sacrament and a once-and-for-all ordinance, Holy Communion is the repeated sacrament in which we are renewed in our baptism and confirmation every time we participate in it.

Holy Communion: The Biblical Basis

On the night that he was betrayed, Jesus ate supper with his disciples in an upstairs room in a private home in Jerusalem. It was a meal with a special purpose. It was to celebrate the Passover.

119

The Passover received its name from God's "passing over" the houses of the Hebrews in Egypt, all of which were marked with the blood of a lamb killed for that purpose, the night that death struck all the firstborn of the Egyptians. (Exod. 12.) The Passover actually had come to mean for the Jews the joyful and thankful remembrance of the whole action of God in delivering them out of Egyptian slavery and leading them through the wilderness to the Promised Land.

Jesus gave a new meaning to the Passover supper in that upper room by taking, blessing, breaking, and giving bread to his disciples, saying that this bread was his body; and by taking a cup of wine, giving thanks, and passing to his disciples, calling it his blood of the new covenant. (Matt. 26; Mark 14; Luke 22.) After the supper, Jesus went to the garden of Gethsemane, and there he prayed the "passion prayer," was betrayed by Judas, and arrested. In less than twenty-four hours, he was reviled, tried, sentenced to death, and hanged upon a cross between two crucified thieves until he died; and his body was taken down from the cross, anointed, enshrouded, and laid in the tomb of Joseph of Arimathea.

On the third day from his death and entombment, Jesus Christ was raised from the dead. On the resurrection day, two of his disciples were going to the village of Emmaus, when Jesus joined them and walked along with them. They did not recognize him, even when "beginning with Moses and all the prophets, he interpreted to them in all the scriptures the things concerning himself" (Luke 24:27.) When they came to Emmaus, the disciples invited their unknown companion to stay with them that night. And

When he was at the table with them, he took bread and blessed, and broke it, and gave it to them. And their eyes were opened and they recognized him; and he vanished out of their sight. They said to each other, "Did not our hearts burn within us while he talked to us on the road, while he opened to us the scriptures?" And they rose that same hour and returned to Jerusalem; and they found the eleven gathered together and those who were with them, who said, "The Lord has risen indeed, and has appeared to Simon!" Then they told what had happened on the road, and how he was known to them in the breaking of the bread. As they were saying this, Jesus himself stood among them.

—Luke 24:30-36

There were, then, two suppers. There was a passion supper and there was a resurrection supper. Between the two suppers, the heart of the great redemptive act in Christ had taken place—the passion-crucifixion-resurrection. It would seem certain that when the disciples came together for further fellowship meals within the week after the Resurrection and thereafter, they remembered *both* suppers with their Lord—the one as he came from his ministry of preaching, teaching, and healing and moved toward his Passion and death; the other as he came from his resurrection and moved toward his ascension and eternal lordship.

The Passion supper meant that the Passover Lamb of the old covenant was now replaced by the Lamb of God of the new covenant. The resurrection supper meant that the Lamb of God was the risen Lord, forever to be among his followers when they should come together "to remember him." The "two suppers become one supper" meant that the atoning sacrifice of God in Christ was at once and inseparably the sanctifying victory of God in Christ!

There is evidence that the early Christians were more mindful of the resurrection emphasis in the fellowship meal than they were of the Passion-crucifixion emphasis. (Acts 2:42-47; Acts 10:41; John 6; John 21; Rev. 3:20.) It even appears that some of them were so overly exuberant in celebrating the resurrection meal that Paul had to remind them that the one who victoriously rose from the dead also was the one who sacrificially died for them and many. (I Cor. 11:17-24.) Therefore, when Christians celebrated the resurrection of the Lord, they also were obligated to remember his Passion and death. The *one supper*—the *one* sacramental, memorial meal—was to be a celebration of profound and serious joy and thanksgiving, for Jesus Christ's death clearly was indispensable to the meaning of Jesus Christ's resurrection. God's "mighty act of redemption in Christ" was "death-resurrection," one and inseparable.

Paul's corrective warning to the Corinthians has obscured to many later Christians the joyful and thankful awareness of Jesus Christ's resurrection and coming again that is an essential aspect of the celebration of Holy Communion. Consequently, the service focused only on the Passion and death often has taken on a somber and rather doleful tone. Paul's word to the Corinthians was needed by them. We also need a word to us. Paul might well say to us, "I would not have you grieve as those who have no hope. Remember that your Lord who suffered and died also rose from the dead! (See I Thess. 4:13-18.) "Do you not know that all of us who have been baptized into Christ Jesus were baptized into his death? We were buried therefore with him by baptism into death, so that as Christ was raised from the dead by the glory of the Father, we too might walk in newness of life." (Romans 6:3-4.) The one great act of redemption that is the meaning of the sacrament of baptism is also the meaning of the sacrament of Holy Communion. Both sacraments, whenever observed, are to be celebrated, giving thanks to God for his gracious gift of life to us through Jesus Christ.

It is likely that the early Christians came together for a sacramental meal within days after the Emmaus supper—certainly not later than the next Sunday. It is not irresponsible fancy to suppose that since the resurrection day itself not a single Sunday has passed when Christians have not come together to celebrate the Supper of their Lord—the Holy Communion—the memorial feast—the great thanksgiving. In fact, since before the end of the first century, A.D., probably not a day has passed without Christians somewhere gathering to do this thing that our Lord commanded to be done in remembrance of him.

Holy Communion: The Service

Quite early in the life of the Church, the service of Holy Communion assumed a simple fourfold form:

1. The offering of bread and wine (the offertory)
2. A prayer of blessing and thanksgiving (the prayer of consecration)
3. The breaking of the bread (the fraction)
4. The distribution of the bread and wine (the distribution or administration of the elements)

The Communion service normally was held with only the full members of the church, "the faithful," in attendance. A different service, consisting of lessons from the holy Scriptures, sermon, prayers, and hymns, was also attended by the faithful as well as by those who were in training to become church members (the catechumens, or those being catechized or instructed.) After a few years, the two services were joined together into one service. After this was done, all those who were not fully members of the church were dismissed just before the offertory, and only "the faithful" remained for the Communion proper.

The service of the early church was developed into fuller services as the years went by, with variations being apparent in the Eastern, or Greek, church and the Western, or Latin, church. Speaking very generally, the Eastern services were lengthier and more elaborate, the emphasis being on the Resurrection as well as on the Passion and Crucifixion. The Western services tended to be simpler, with the emphasis being quite largely on the sacrificial death of the Lord.

Our own Methodist service is rooted in the Western tradition. The service of Salisbury Cathedral (the *Sarum Missal*) was the basis used by Archbishop Cranmer in shaping the first Protestant (Anglican) service in England. With the *Sarum Missal* as the core, Cranmer drew from Lutheran and Greek Orthodox services to design this first Anglican service in 1549. This service was revised in 1552, 1559, 1604, and 1662. The 1662 revision also drew on the Scottish service of 1637. In 1784, John Wesley abridged the 1662 Book of Common Prayer of the Church of England, made a few changes and additions, and entitled it *The Sunday Service of the Methodists in North America,* and sent it over for use in this country. From the Communion service in *The Sunday Service,* all the American Methodist services have come. The Methodist Episcopal Church made revisions in 1792 and 1844. After the two separations, the Methodist Episcopal Church, the Methodist Episcopal Church, South, and the Methodist Protestant Church revised their services from time to time, drawing on each other. After reunion in 1939, two services were provided for alternative use in The Methodist Church. The 1964 service of Holy Communion of The Methodist Church is intended to be evangelical in content and spirit, a thankful celebration of the whole gospel of Jesus Christ—one which at once embodies the meanings of the passion supper and the resurrection supper.

Christians call their sacramental meal by several names—the Lord's Supper, the Mass, the Holy Communion, the Holy Liturgy, the Holy Eucharist. While each name carries its own characteristic emphasis, the same basic content is found under each name.

We may spell out this basic content as:

1. Remembrance
2. Proclamation

3. Offertory
4. Participation
5. Thanksgiving

We cannot say that one basic aspect is essential and the others are of secondary importance. Rather, each aspect may be thought of as an arc of a circle; if one arc is omitted or shortened, then the circle no longer exists. In its stead, there is only a broken curved line which at best may be only suggestive of a circle. Therefore, a full and sound service of Holy Communion is the entire service which adequately expresses all five aspects of the basic content.

Remembrance

"In remembrance of me"—these well may be the most familiar of all the words that are related to the Lord's Supper. These words appear on thousands of altars and communion tables across Methodism, reminding us that what we do in this sacrament is done in obedience to the Lord's own command, "Do this in remembrance of me." In the oldest account of the Jerusalem supper (I Cor. 11: 23-26), Jesus is said to have given this command twice—once in connection with the bread and once in connection with the wine.

But *who* is it that we remember? We remember more than a young prophet on the night before his death. We remember that he was more than a prophet, for we are put in mind of his birth when angels sang their song of glory; of his baptism when God expressed his pleasure in his well-beloved Son; and of his words of teaching and deeds of healing when men marveled at what he said and did. We remember more—so much more than what we remember cannot be contained within the usual meaning of "remembrance." It is more nearly "revealed awareness" than simply "remembrance." For we are aware, by God's revelation, that the Lord whose command we obey is the pre-existent Word who was with God in the beginning, who was God, and through whom

125

God made all things (John 1:1-5); the Incarnate God, wholly God and wholly man; the obedient Son of God in his baptism, preaching, teaching, and healing as well as in his passion and death; the representative Son of man, representing us all in his temptation, suffering, death, and resurrection; the atoning Messiah, the Lamb of God, in his Passion, crucifixion, and death; the mighty Savior in his resurrection; the Lord of lords, Kings of kings, and heavenly Advocate in his ascension and eternal rulership; and the Judge of all men in his coming again.

The second coming, in its essence, means that God will at last complete through Jesus Christ the redemptive victory which he has begun through Jesus Christ. Creation and second coming are "God's great acts" of the beginning and the end—the Alpha and the Omega—and the meaning of it all is caught up in the birth, obedient life, Passion, crucifixion, resurrection, and ascension of the One whom we remember as we celebrate together the sacred meal.

The Lord's Supper, then, is no simple "memorial" centering on the Lord's death. It is a wondrous remembrance, a revealed awareness, of God's purpose in Christ in creation and coming again, whereby our lives in the present have meaning and hope.

Proclamation

Paul said, "For as often as you eat this bread and drink this cup, you proclaim the Lord's death until he comes." (I Cor. 11:26.) To "proclaim" is to "set forth strongly and clearly"; it is to "bear witness with confident assurance."

That which is proclaimed—"the Lord's death until he comes"—stands for the whole person and work of Jesus Christ. To say "he died for us" is to mean "he gave his life for us." So the whole meaning of Jesus' death includes all that we mean by the remembrance of him. Therefore, when Christians celebrate the Holy

126

Communion, they proclaim the whole gospel of Jesus Christ, both to themselves and to all men.

As a specific act, the Holy Communion is our principal witness to the gospel. It is sound and right that every celebration of this sacrament should include a lesson or lessons from the holy Scriptures and a sermon, as well as an offertory; prayers of praise, confession, intercession, consecration, commitment and thanksgiving; and the distributing and partaking of the bread and the wine. In the whole service of Holy Communion, the *whole* gospel is proclaimed—the entire meaning of "the Lord's death until he comes."

Offertory

At the heart of the Christian faith, there is a mystery. The mystery is a Person. The Person is at once divine and human—truly God and truly man. He is Jesus Christ. This is the witness of the church in the holy Scriptures and in the historic creeds.

The Christian mystery is an offense to the human mind trying to act of itself, simply because mystery cannot be contained within rational sense. The Christian mystery is the greatest of all blessings to human faith because this mystery is revelation, meaning, and hope, and indeed makes living sense. (I Cor. 1:18-25.) The Christian testifies that he knows God only through Jesus Christ, and that he knows himself only through Jesus Christ. So in his work of revelation Jesus Christ reveals God as he is and man as he ought to be and may become. But more than this: Jesus Christ is God's offertory of his redemptive love to men, and at the same time Jesus Christ is man's offertory of perfect obedience to God.

One way to look at the whole meaning of the Holy Communion is as the celebration of the great double offertory—God's offering of himself to men through Christ; men offering of themselves to God through Christ.

Offertory thus conceived is the real meaning of Christian sacrifice. Sacrifice is willing, purposeful self-giving. Jesus Christ is, "by the one offering of himself, a full, perfect, and sufficient sacrifice for the sins of the whole world." This is God's sacrifice—his willing, purposeful giving of himself for the sake of his children. At the same time, Jesus Christ is the one through whom we offer to God "ourselves, our souls and bodies, to be a reasonable, holy and lively sacrifice" unto him.

Methodists are accustomed to emphasizing the rededication of their lives to God in the sacrament of Holy Communion. A genuinely Christian rededication involves us in the "great offertory." We can offer to God our hearts and the fruits of the labor of our hands only as we accept his offering of redemptive love through Jesus Christ, and in turn make our offering to God through the same Jesus Christ, our Savior and our Lord.

It is the Holy Spirit who enables us to accept God's offertory of saving love. It is the Holy Spirit who enables us to offer ourselves to God in response to his love and to know the blessedness of being accepted by him, thus being renewed in our relationship to him as his children who desire above all else to do his will. The great offertory, then, is completed as the Holy Spirit, the divine guiding and sustaining Power, goes with us into our daily work, our homes, and our civic and social activities, thereby making possible our continuing response to God in joyful obedience to him in all our living.

Participation

"The cup of blessing which we bless, is it not a participation in the blood of Christ? The bread which we break, is it not a participation in the body of Christ? Because there is one loaf, we who are many are one body, for we all partake of the same loaf." (I Cor. 10:16-17.)

Because we participate in Jesus Christ, because we are related to the human nature of Jesus Christ in a mystical and real way, we can claim his righteousness and his perfect obedience to God as representing us. He has done for us that which we could not do for ourselves by his Incarnation, his life, death, resurrection, and ascension: he has effected our forgiveness which we now are to accept and live.

The heart of participation in the Holy Communion is the acceptance of Jesus Christ's gift of salvation. As we accept his gift, we are reconciled to God and to one another. (Romans 5:6-11.) We are made to know that we are members of the great company of believers of all time—those who have gone before and those who will come after, as well as those of our own day. So it is that in the celebration of the Lord's Supper we praise God "with angels and archangels and with all the company of heaven." This is the *Holy Communion*—the being in community of living faith with God and with all fellow Christians. This is the celebration of restoration to the relationship with God and men that was God's very purpose for us in creation. Consequently, redemption *from* sin (sin, which is self-centeredness and estrangement at its heart) is redemption *to* God's "creation-purpose" which will at last be realized in the coming again. Through Jesus Christ we are made participants in God's victory.

Thanksgiving

Sometimes the prayers in the service of Holy Communion, beginning with "Lift up your hearts" (the *Sursum Corda*), and continuing through the prayer of consecration, are called "the great thanksgiving." It is thanksgiving for the great offertory, for the One remembered, for the proclaimed gospel, for participation in the death and resurrection and ascension of Jesus Christ. The thanksgiving looks with confident hope to the messianic banquet—the Holy

Communion of all his children with God when he will complete the victorious redemption.

Every observance of this sacrament, then, is a thankful celebration of God's redemptive work through Jesus Christ. The term "eucharist" means "thanksgiving." Charles Wesley almost always referred to the Holy Communion as the Holy Eucharist, and John Wesley frequently did so. "Eucharist" is especially compatible with the Methodist spirit of joyful, experienced salvation. It would be well if present-day Methodists should recover both the term and the spirit.

John Wesley's whispered words on his deathbed, "I'll praise, I'll praise," are recalled for us by Umphrey Lee in his last book, *Our Fathers and Us: The Heritage of the Methodists.*[6] These are the first words of Watts' hymn which begins:

> I'll praise my Maker while I've breath,
> And when my voice is lost in death,
>   Praise shall employ my nobler powers;
> My days of praise shall ne'er be past,
> While life, and thought, and being last,
>   Or Immortality endures.

Lee goes on then to speak of Christian in *Pilgrim's Progress* who, when he

had divested himself of his mortal garments he heard the sound of trumpets, and when Mr. Valiant-for-truth passed over "all the trumpets sounded for him on the other side."

These are great words, among the greatest in our Christian heritage. But I should like most humbly to suggest that the contribution of the Methodists to a changing world was largely in their belief that they on this side of the dark waters caught the sound of trumpets.[7]

[6] (Dallas: S. M. U. Press, 1958).
[7] *Ibid,* p. 113.

It is in the Holy Communion that the heart most completely celebrates even now the final victory of God for which "the trumpet shall sound" (I Cor. 15:52-57), and this with a joyful thanksgiving that makes meeting with the song of the morning stars at creation, the glory hymn of the angels on the birthnight of the Lord, and the *Sanctus* of the heavenly creatures around the eternal throne of God, when the whole creation will have been redeemed to God's perfect will through Jesus Christ.

The Holy Communion is the great continuing revival in which we remember our Savior; proclaim his whole gospel; participate in the great offertory; and give thanks to God for the wonder of his redeeming love in Jesus Christ, that we, even we, "should be called the sons of God!" (I John 3:1.)

Chapter 6

WEDDINGS AND FUNERALS

Since Christian worship is the celebration by the church of the whole gospel of Jesus Christ, each service of worship contains this wholeness, even when the major emphasis is on a particular phase of the gospel. We see this on particular days such as Christmas and Easter, when we celebrate the Incarnation and Resurrection as these events relate to the whole message of God's good news in Jesus Christ. In a sense, therefore, Christian worship is not only a celebration and affirmation of the *timeless,* but also each service of the church is a celebration in the *timely.* The demand for relevance comes from both the eternal and the temporal. Weddings and funerals are two such distinctive instances which confront the Christian with the demands of the gospel, yet often are in tension with the secular culture in which we live.

Our study of both weddings and funerals will move from the assumption that they are occasions when the church congregates for worship, and is called to rejoice in the whole gospel under unique circumstances.

The Wedding

Unlike the custom in many other nations, in the United States the church marriage ceremony is recognized by both the church and the state as being the only service required. In a sense, therefore, the minister is, for this time, an officer representing both the church in particular and society in general as the chief witness to the validity of the marriage. Such a role by the minister is a relatively recent development in Christian history, for neither the synagogue nor the early church offers us a tradition for the wedding as a religious service.

From the Roman customs there come the public betrothal, the ring and other presents, the joining of hands, the kiss. In early Roman practice the wedding proper took place at a later time. The giving away of the bride was a custom which came from northern Europe. It was not until the eleventh century that the priest presided over the betrothal as well as the nuptial Eucharist and blessing.[1]

Though some churches require the publishing of the banns to the congregation prior to the wedding, this is not done in most denominations. With the increasing training of ministers as counselors and the instability of the American home, as represented in part by a very high rate of divorce, there is an increasing demand upon couples to plan their wedding in such a way that they can take advantage of all the church has to offer in helping establish an "enduring home."

---

[1] See Massey Hamilton Shepherd, Jr., *The Oxford American Prayer Book Commentary* (New York: Oxford University Press, 1950), for a brief and helpful history of the marriage ceremony.

In all services of various Christian churches the bride and groom marry each other, and are, in a very real sense, the ministers of the service. The presence of a minister, however, as well as witnesses from the congregation, attests to the fact that a wedding is not a service involving the decision of just two persons. The church and society have a great stake in their decision, and do retain the right to give or withhold their blessing. Most of the major denominations are giving close study to their rules in regard to marriage in order not to relax the demands placed upon the couple, but to make these demands contribute to the stability of the home in a rapidly changing culture.

The Wedding Ceremony [2]

The wedding ceremony itself is necessarily restricted as a service of Christian worship. Though it is corporate in the sense that a community assembles, it is particularized as it centers upon the marriage commitment of the two principal persons. The normative service in most English-speaking Protestant churches is the "Form of Solemnization of Matrimony" from the Book of Common Prayer. The general movement of the service varies little from ritual to ritual.

The service begins with a drawing together of the people, and comes to a climax with the arrival of the bride and groom. The minister then reads a paragraph that states the purpose of the gathering of the church, which is actually a call to worship. This opening statement gives the foundation of the church's belief in the godly institution of marriage. Many such statements quote from Jesus and Paul to show the biblical foundation of the home. Several modern services have eliminated some of these quotations, probably because most Protestant churches do not consider the wedding as a sacrament and do not demand the "dominical institution" from

[2] (It is suggested that a copy of a wedding ritual be read prior to reading this section.)

Scripture. However, the opening paragraph is a clear statement to all who are present that marriage is "instituted of God" and thus should be entered into "reverently, discreetly, and in the fear of God." Older forms of the marriage ceremony gave a long and specific list of the purposes of marriage, but these have been largely eliminated.

Following this general statement to the congregation, the service moves to a more specific exhortation and charge to the particular man and woman who have come to be joined. This charge varies widely in many services, but in each case it states very specifically to the bride and groom the nature of the affirmation they are to make before God and the people.

The minister then, on behalf of the church and society, asks the intentions first of the man and then of the woman toward marriage with each other. If these questions are answered affirmatively, then the bride is "given away" to the groom by her father or some other person she may choose. The father or the one substituting for him *represents* the family of the bride in this act, and properly replies simply, "I do," to the question, "Who giveth this woman to be married to this man?"

It is at this point that the couple become the real ministers of the service. Having accepted the church's view of marriage and stated publicly their desire to be responsible partners, they join hands and declare to each other before God their deepest commitment of faith. These declarations to each other are probably the most unequivocal statements in the English language. They contain no conditional clauses.

The giving and receiving of rings follow these pledges as outward signs or symbols of the vows which have been made.

The rituals often vary the order of the service following the giving of the rings, but each contains the pronouncement of the

135

couple as husband and wife, and the prayer or prayers on their behalf and the Lord's Prayer said by all. The service ends with the blessing of God pronounced by the minister.

The Wedding as Worship

In what sense is the marriage service a celebration by the church of the whole gospel? To answer the question tempts one to force a rationale for this service of holy matrimony into a pattern of full Christain worship which may lead to an indefensible position. In its own particular emphasis, however, the service contains strong elements of the recognition of God in the context of marriage and the family. The judgment of God upon our lives and the affirmation of ourselves as finite persons under God's merciful redemption are expressed throughout the service. The central acts of commitment contain the elements of offertory and thanksgiving; and the prayers of praise, petition, intercession, and dedication bring a completeness to the service which is characteristic of all services of Christian worship.

Though few churches believe the wedding to be a sacrament, the service is sacramental in its essential meaning. This is evident particularly in the acts and symbols used. The giving away, the joining of hands, the giving and receiving of rings, the blessings upon the couple, and a kiss all attest the faith that God uses our acts and signs to become means of making his presence known.

Frequently, there are couples who wish to strengthen the sense of worship within the framework of the service. The singing of congregational hymns, the reading of scriptures, and the preaching of a short sermon are often elements in a service of Christian marriage. The observance of Holy Communion as the first act of worship following the wedding sometimes is done. Real questions may be raised about the advisability of a Communion service which does not include all those gathered, yet the particular nature of a marriage service may make this limited participation justifiable.

Christian Worship and Social Customs

A couple planning their wedding soon find many influences being felt, some of which will be in sharp conflict with one another. Nowhere is this revealed more keenly than in relation to music and decorations.

Though one would be hard put to identify music as such with the sacred or secular, society identifies its music as being fitting only for certain occasions by its traditional use and the words that often accompany the music. On the other hand, the local customs often sanction the use of some music at weddings which traditionally has been identified with anything but Christian worship. The "traditional" wedding marches are rapidly losing their traditional place, partly because their origin is far removed from Christian worship on the one hand, and partly because there are far more suitable compositions available on the other. Vocal music appropriate for weddings must be judged by both music and words. No one would deny that romance is an important aspect of marriage, but romantic songs do not represent the profound nature of marriage and are hardly conducive to worship. Yet there are often local customs that permit and encourage the use of unsuitable songs which are in violent disagreement with Christian worship. One is seriously tempted here to recite bad examples, yet it would be better to refer to pamphlets which several denominations (especially Episcopal and Methodist) make available, listing suitable music for weddings.

Often local customs permit or encourage "contests" in church decoration. Such a festival occasion as a wedding ought to be reflected in the atmosphere of the church building, but always within the discipline of Christian worship. All church decorations should

137

be used to enhance the distinctive Christian symbols in the church. Any decorations which detract from the major symbols of worship should be considered unnecessary ostentation which detracts from worship rather than enhances it. This may be applied to flowers and greenery, candles, and the clothes worn by the wedding party. The happiness and joy which characterize a wedding are considerably more Christian when restrained within the framework of the solemnity of the worship of God.

Perhaps a parenthetical word may be added here to ask for the right of non-Christian couples to have a pagan festival of marriage which meets the communities' standards in some suitable hall without asking either the couple or the church to participate in a lie. A couple should not be forced by society to go through the motions of a service of Christian worship when neither one of them believes the Christian faith which is the foundation of the service. Nor should the church and its ministers be forced into the role of conducting a pagan service in the sanctuary. Society's demand for a wedding performed within the church without consideration of the church or the couple is placing both in a vulnerable position.

The wedding of two Christians is an occasion for the whole community of faith to celebrate the union in a joyous service of solemn worship—or a solemn service of joyous worship. This commitment between any two persons which holds such significance for the whole of the church and society for generations to come demands our very best thought and planning. The vows may be made in the presence of a few guests or in the midst of hundreds. In either case, it properly is a service of the worship of God as he is revealed in Jesus Christ, and it therefore contains the highest offering to him— the self-giving of two persons to God in their new oneness with each other. This offering is expressed by word and act within the service itself, and is expressed by living in the home which is established by God through this service.

The Funeral

The death of a member of a church is a call to worship. Here the living are confronted with stark reality which calls all Christians to their understanding of life and death. But vast differences exist in this understanding, and no service of Christian worship is under greater tensions from many sides than the funeral. One not confronted with a death at the moment may be glib about the Christian message concerning death, but in actually planning a service of worship for a particular death, many factors come quickly to the surface.

Quite aside from the teachings of the church, there are numerous local customs and mores which have no foundation in the Christian faith. The actual disposition or preservation of the body varies widely among Christians. The display of the body is a common practice in many places, and unheard of in others. The attention placed on the body may be an offense to many, whereas to others, the lack of concern for the body may be a scandal. Some customs surrounding the event of death dictate that funerals shall come soon after death; others, that there will be several days before the funeral service. More recent trends in urban life have affected funeral customs sharply. The church and home have, in the majority of cases, now been supplanted by the "funeral chapel" as the place of the service in most cities. In an earlier day the majority of the community gathered for the service; today fewer and fewer persons take time to attend burial services. Professional funeral directors and musicians have given the services "polish" that makes them quite different from the way they were in an earlier and more rural setting. But there is no disposition here to do more than call attention to some of the changes with which our day must reckon.

More fundamental than these changes, however, are the changes which have come among Christians as they examine death in the

139

light of their faith. The chances of anyone of us believing what our grandparents, or even our parents, believe or believed about death are slim indeed. Even if our faith is not too different, the symbols we use to communicate this faith have undergone radical changes. Listen to a discussion among a group of Christians about death and one will soon discover some of the differences between 1900 and today. Few such discussions reach easily agreed upon answers, and a more characteristic result is confusion and uncertainty. This is not to suggest that such discussions should not take place, but rather to point up the greater need for more serious study by Christians in local churches.

Ministers themselves discuss funerals as services which often do more to violate the Christian faith than affirm it, yet there is no clear word spoken that offers much encouragement. There are so many influences which tend to turn us aside from the reality of death itself. A false use of the Bible has been employed to gloss over the reality of the end of this flesh. Such sentimentality often compounds grief and leaves little room for the affirmation of the Christian faith. If death is indeed a call to worship, how shall the church respond as it comes together for this worship?

As in all services of worship, this particular occasion makes certain demands. In the event of death the demands of grief, mystery, loss, drastic change, and questioned faith call us to the Word of God for comfort and for strength in Jesus Christ. The church calls its members together at the funeral, not only to celebrate the gospel, but to hear it again in the midst of many unanswered questions. Christians collect at the death of a fellow member, not because they know no doubts and fears, but precisely because they need the reaffirmation of their faith and trust when this faith and trust is most severely tested.

The attitudes of the people toward the deceased one will vary at different funerals. There are often services where the one who has died has reached the end of a long life, death is expected and, in a sense, is a fitting end. There are many deaths, however, which seem untimely and often tragic. In any case, the living are confronted again with the mystery of life itself. The church responds to this call to worship by standing together before the Giver of life and death and affirming that "if we live, we live to the Lord, and if we die, we die to the Lord; so then, whether we live or whether we die, we are the Lord's." (Romans 14:8.)

The Funeral Service

The rituals for the funeral usually follow a common pattern. Most of them start with verses of scripture which really are calls to worship and which contain the promises of God's mercy and presence. In fact, the entire service is predominantly readings from the Bible. This strong emphasis on well-chosen scripture is the church's way of standing in and before the Word of God, that it may speak its own message to those assembled. The same selections from the psalms, the Gospels, and the epistles, which are generally found in all rituals, are also suggested for use in the ritual of The Methodist Church.

The responses of the people to this Word are customarily in the form of prayers. A characteristic of an increasing number of funerals today is that of giving the people an opportunity to respond. The participation of the congregation in singing great hymns of praise and affirmation, the *Gloria Patri,* saying a creed, or in praying the great prayers of the church are some of the best means available to us for Christian worship at a funeral.

The preaching of a sermon is strongly recommended for the funeral, provided the term "sermon" is clearly understood. In the context of a funeral it is important to let the sermon be very brief—perhaps about five minutes. But even in these few minutes there

141

can be this contemporary witness of the faith under these particular circumstances. This is not to suggest a eulogy of the person being buried; rather, this is to be a proclamation of the gospel as another means for the grace of God in its judgment and mercy to be made known. It is another word of faith and affirmation which has characterized Christian worship through the centuries. It is dangerous to mention the sermon for fear it will suggest the addresses which are more suitable at memorial services, or sermons which seem to satisfy the desire of the preacher to speak to those he does not often see in his congregation. Excesses of this kind have led many thoughtful ministers to eliminate the sermon from the funeral service altogether. It is fortunate that the choices are not limited just to these two extremes.

The prayers within the service are a response by the people, whether they are read together or said on behalf of the congregation by the minister. They should be prayers of praise, thanksgiving, petition, intercession, and dedication. The prayers, like the whole service, should be brief; yet they should be an offering from the people to God in faith and trust.

The committal of the body is a symbol of the offering of life itself and is an act of reverence, love, and faith. Many rituals have placed undue emphasis on the dead body, while others fail to recognize the reality of the body and its death. The Greeks, with their teachings of the immortality of the soul, have often been more influential here than the Hebrews and early Christians. The unity of God's creation does not permit us to be either flippant about our bodies or to fool ourselves about our mortality. At the side of a grave the church stands in trust before the eternal God who holds all time—past, present, and future—in his good care. It is he who gives us the life which must end, and it is he who offers us in Christ life which is eternal.

The service of committal, therefore, is an act which is done with as few words as possible, as reverently and quietly as possible; it is not a time for exhortation but a time to act in faith.

The entire service is for the entire congregation. Those who are most closely touched by the death certainly become of major concern. The pastoral responsibility rests upon the minister and the people in their recognition of the grief caused by this particular death. Grief demands expression as does faith, and a funeral service which ignores either is unrealistic. On the other hand, there ought to be nothing in the service of worship which is a direct appeal to an expression of grief. The use of sentimental songs and poems and undue personal references have no place in a Christian funeral. It is also widely felt that viewing the body by the congregation at the close of the service is not helpful to the family or the friends. There are usually times prior to the service of worship when the body may be seen in private.

Local customs vary widely in the use of flowers in a service. It would seem fitting that the use of flowers should enhance the setting of worship rather than become a floral display. Certainly flowers should never cover or hide the chief symbols of the church building.

The sending of flowers has long been a means of expressing our love and sympathy to friends who have lost a member of the family. On the other hand, it can be a way to avoid the difficulty of a more personal expression. But the flowers which mean so much as expressions of love may better be used at the grave or in the home rather than in the church. At the church the places normally used for flowers certainly may be utilized.

Other Occasional Services

In the corporate life of the church there are special times which call for extraordinary services of worship. Our rituals provide suggested services for these occasions, which may include the dedication of particular persons or groups or things in the church. Worship services of this sort are quite fitting, but they are of such a particular nature that no attempt will be made here to discuss them in detail. But whether a church is dedicating one of its members for a particular job, or a group of church officers, or a new organ, it may very well be included in the regular worship of the church or a special service may be planned. If it is a special service, care should be taken by the minister and the appropriate committee to make the service a faithful celebration of the gospel as it relates particularly to the special occasion. That we gather at the call of God to worship him is an especially important fact to remember. On special occasions we tend to place so much emphasis on the persons or things which are the objects of our interest that God, in whose name we meet, is often ignored. This is vividly illustrated on many markers, where "to the glory of God" is in very small letters and the name of the one honored is in huge letters. Let all services of Christian worship be for the glorification of God under all circumstances.

To Those Who Conduct the Services

When the church gathers for worship at weddings or funerals or on other occasions, the attitude of all the worshipers is of great importance, but the minister has been trained by the church as the servant who leads the people in this worship. Thus the minister, as a servant of the gospel, always is a servant of the people. His crucial position certainly does not give him the power to make people worship or refrain from worshiping, yet in a contradictory sense the attitude of the minister is a dominant force here. People are made aware of God by God himself, but he uses persons most of the time to effect this awareness. A minister who is worshiping when he conducts a wedding or funeral is very likely to make himself a

144

means for others to worship. On the other hand, a minister who has become a machine for conducting services becomes something for both God and the people to overcome.

The work of the minister calls neither for the "shrinking violet" nor the "drill sergeant." It does call for one who is there to celebrate the gospel and who is well prepared to fulfill the work of leading others in this celebration. Years of preparation have made it possible for him to speak and act so as to be a "means of grace."

Each service becomes a new service. This particular wedding or that particular funeral demands the most careful planning. It is not easy to avoid the danger of becoming so dulled by the same service over and over again that the prayers and other acts of worship become mere rote. Such a mechanized minister has died, though his funeral may be delayed for many years. Sharing in the joys of a wedding by becoming freshly aware of the meanings in this service for these particular persons is a drain on one's emotions. Living within the grief of a family who knows death is a temptation to a minister to wear the mask of faith and never be touched in his own soul; but he is called of God to be a participant in the midst of the life of his people, not a robot who only recites the appropriate words.

Let the minister lead the service as one who worships and in so doing he becomes a vehicle for the church gathered to do the same. Thereby, the ritual performs its proper function as it becomes a means of worship for all those who participate in its service.

Chapter 7

THE SYMBOLS AND SETTING OF OUR WORSHIP

God gives us all that we have. In worship we render thanks to him for all his benefits. We use some of the very gifts God has given us in the act of praying and thanking him for all that he has done for us. The talents which we use to perform our worship are God-given. This is true of the skills which have gone into building and furnishing our churches. "We give thee but thine own," but we nevertheless are called upon to offer our worship to God. Christianity, then, does not seek to abandon material things in its worship, since they too are gifts of God. Our worship is "in spirit and truth," and the use of physical things helps it to be so.

Historically, Protestants have maintained that "no place is capable of any holiness" nor do things have any sanctity in themselves. Their sanctity comes through their function. Thus Protestants are not inconsistent when they speak of the church building as a sanctuary; they simply are attributing sacred uses to the building. When art and architecture are used to help men perform their work of common worship, their liturgy, they have a sacred function. We speak of liturgical art and liturgical architecture in referring to the works of art and the buildings which have this sacred function.

The Nature of Liturgical Art

Not all religious art is liturgical art, since only a small portion of religious art is intended for use in Christian worship. The difference is largely one of function. Much of the religious art with which we would adorn our homes, our classrooms, and other places has no direct relationship to our worship. A painting of the good Samaritan we find edifying, but we would be unlikely to use it in our worship. In performing "our bounden duty" of worship some tools are necessary, and the utility of them may be enhanced by painting, sculpture, stained glass, and other art forms. Thus liturgical art is found in the furnishings of churches, the Communion vessels, the altar utensils, paintings, and pieces of sculpture. This is art which has a function in worship. It is much more than a matter of decoration, since the articles themselves have an utilitarian purpose in worship.

The purpose of all liturgical art is to make us conscious of the presence of the divine in our worship. We know that God is present in the midst of those gathered to worship him, yet at the same time we do not know it. Liturgical art helps us to be conscious of the presence of God, who is unseen. There is a parallel in the experience of the disciples on the Emmaus road. Christ was in their midst, but it took one of his characteristic actions, the breaking of bread, to make them aware of his presence. In liturgical

147

art we are helped to recognize the presence of God, who is in our midst. Liturgical art does not make God present. It does, however, make us aware of his presence. In a sense, photographs of loved ones give us a feeling of their presence, though we know that they are elsewhere. Liturgical art helps us realize the actual presence of God, who always remains unseen.

Having said this, it is necessary to remind ourselves of the great witness Protestantism has borne to the fact that God can never be confused with physical objects. The Old Testament scoffs at the pagan worshipers who adored wooden idols which could be used to more practical effect as firewood. The adoration of carved or molded images was severely condemned. In all this the purpose was in making it clear that God can never be identified with any purely physical object. The universe is his and he made it, but he can never be confused with it. Liturgical art is like a direction marker which points to a town but can never be confused with the town itself. It is a means to an end and must always be distinguished from that end.

Liturgical art, then, must always point beyond itself, since its function is not to attract attention to itself but to one who is greater than all the universe. Our interest is not in nature and natural objects for themselves. We worship the God who creates and redeems nature. Thus our liturgical art must always go beyond the surface appearance of things as they exist. It cannot be content with what is simply apparent; always it pushes us on to the meaning behind the obvious. Good liturgical art can never merely mimic the photographer; it must probe beneath things as they seem to things as they are. Much of the art which decorates Sunday-school rooms is incapable of serving as liturgical art since it is so obvious. Jesus was a man—true—but liturgical art says more than this. It shows something of the awesome majesty of the divine presence in Jesus the Christ. Liturgical art helps us to worship by conveying to our senses something of the numinous character of the Godhead clothed in the flesh of Jesus of Nazareth. It helps us to worship because it goes beyond representation and becomes interpretation. Jesus was man, but he is also the Christ whom we worship. Liturgical art serves to keep us conscious of this.

Besides this quality of spiritual depth, liturgical art has other characteristics which differentiate it from religious art in general. Cyril Richardson distinguishes liturgical art from other art in three ways: by liturgical art's use of traditional symbols, by its communal nature, and by its religious power.

Christianity is a specific faith with certain common beliefs and history. Liturgical art cannot ignore the received tradition of Christian symbols. Through the passage of twenty centuries various symbols have become so eloquent with meaning that they cannot be superseded. The figure of the cross; the action of breaking bread; kneeling or bowing for prayer—all these are symbols which we cherish. These traditional symbolic images and actions have inexhaustible possibilities of expression which novel symbols could not readily duplicate. The traditional images say something to the whole Christian community, for they have grown out of its life. As a rule, liturgical art does not seek originality in subject matter, but avoids it.

Liturgical art works for the Christian community, and therefore is not individualistic. It seeks to express what has meaning for all, not simply for the scholar or artist. It must have power to communicate to the whole church. Some symbols have become dead. To most contemporary Christians peacocks and pomegranates do not suggest anything more than birds or fruits. These symbols no longer communicate, though they spoke of immortality and the Resurrection to early Christians. One of the problems facing Protestantism today is that so many of the old symbols no longer have meaning and the life of our Christian community has not yet replaced them. Individuals cannot produce new symbols; they come out of the life of the whole community, and this is a slow process. The artist expresses what the church feels, and he must know the mind of the church before he can create liturgical art.

Far more important than the aesthetic quality of liturgical art is its religious power. Matters of style are secondary compared to the dimension of depth. Does the work of art express the presence of the Infinite through its use of finite matter? Then it has the qualities of liturgical art however unsophisticated the artist may be in matters of technique. Liturgical art was not intended for museums. It has far different criteria from those which satisfy an art critic. Its function is of great importance in a religion at whose heart is the Incarnation. Liturgical art seeks to make us conscious of the presence of a God who creates, uses, and redeems the people and the things of this world.

Liturgical Art in Protestantism

During the Middle Ages liturgical art reached a state of high development. The typical medieval church was a treasure house of both liturgical art, the art utilized in common worship, and devotional art, the art used for personal devotions. As devotions changed —and they seem to change more frequently than the liturgy—new devotional objects were added. The medieval worshiper in his devotions could contemplate the terrors of the day of judgment, meditate on the agonies of Christ on the way to Calvary, or reflect upon the acts of biblical figures and the saints. Liturgical art adorned all the items used in the Mass, including the vestments of the priests, the utensils used upon the altar, the vessel in which the consecrated host was kept, and the other furnishings of the building. All about were painted, carved, and glazed figures of the saints and angels. The purpose of all this art was to bring the believer into the presence of the holy, since it was believed that Christ was tabernacled among his people in the consecrated host. Everything spoke of the divine Victim sacrificed upon the altar whose presence filled the church.

The Protestant Reformers of the sixteenth century were not of one mind about the liturgical art which they inherited from medieval Catholicism. Some of the Reformers found medieval liturgical art fraught with peril; others found much of it indifferent or even agreeable. Luther tended to be more conservative, relishing much liturgical art when it did not directly conflict with his doctrines. Zwingli and others removed paintings, statues, vestments, and other objects of art from their churches. In England and Scotland great quantities of liturgical art were destroyed during the sixteenth century.

To us this sounds a bit unnecessary, but we forget the power which liturgical art had for the Christian of the sixteenth century. It possessed powers for mediating the divine Presence. There was danger, the Reformers felt, in that ignorant people sometimes mistook the object for that which it represented. The church could say that one only reverenced the subject represented in reverencing an image, but could the layman always remember this distinction? Furthermore, of what use were representations of the saints if one did not depend upon the intercession of the saints? The core of the matter was a fear that liturgical art might confuse the divine and the natural. It might become idolatrous. God was the only object of man's worship, and no symbols were adequate to express his majesty and glory.

And so many Protestants felt it necessary to destroy the crucifixes, the vessels, and the altars of medieval churches. They destroyed them, not because they opposed art, but because they took it so seriously. For the art of the time was potent, full of power to convey the presence of the holy. It was not something to be admired in museums, but an active thing doing its work in the churches. When

151

it was doing the wrong work, when people attributed the power to an object rather than to what it represented, the Reformation demanded its destruction. The sixteenth-century Catholic might destroy medieval art to replace it with the contemporary renaissance art; the Protestant destroyed art because it challenged his theology.

Had the Reformation occurred two centuries later, this destruction might not have been necessary. Increasingly the mind of eighteenth-century man divorced the natural and the divine. God had created the world, but to many it seemed that he had become somewhat emeritus thereafter. The world might be compared to a wonderful watch, marvelously made; but after God had wound it up, it went on ticking without his interference. The implications of this for art were clear. Art was simply the manipulation of natural objects to represent other natural objects. Since it was entirely rational and explicable, there was no need to fear its power. Men were too enlightened to entertain such apparent superstitions. Art lost its numinous quality, and for many people it has never had any since. The eighteenth century produced much less religious art in the Protestant countries. The art that went into the churches was often simply representations of cherubs, fruit, and other decorations not intended to be vehicles of the divine. As far as mediating the divine Presence was concerned, such art was dead. It could be hung in art galleries where landscapes, nudes, and crucifixions could be compared as artistic compositions.

Since art was so thoroughly safe, Protestants lost their fear of it. The nineteenth century brought a great deal of nostalgia for the past, and this was reflected in Protestant churches as well as elsewhere. The Middle Ages proved to be most intriguing, and countless Protestant churches were built in various styles of Gothic architecture. The effect for which these buildings strived demanded full employment of the arts, especially stained glass and painting. Many Protestants simply copied medieval buildings, including the art of the Middle Ages. There was no reason why they should not since they did not consider art capable of conveying the power of the supernatural. Instead, the skill with which much nineteenth-century painting and stained glass imitated nature attracted many Protestants to use those means for teaching morals and illustrating biblical themes.

American Protestants in the twentieth century, along with the rest of our society, have become increasingly sophisticated and prosperous. We welcome art into our churches without foreboding today. But most of it is used simply to decorate. Our churches show a willingness to use stained glass, colored hangings, paintings, and carved figures. We use symbols constantly in the decoration of the building. Frequently a congregation which has erected a new church building publishes a pamphlet to explain the symbolism with which the church is ornamented. There is real irony here. The symbolism has to be interpreted for the congregation. But if it really grew out of the life of the community of faith it certainly would need no such explantion. Most of such symbolism is of an obscure or antiquarian nature, and communicates nothing to the congregation upon whom it is imposed.

But art is not now what it was in the eighteenth and nineteenth centuries. The genuine artist today feels constrained to go beyond reproducing things as they appear to the eye—after all, the camera can do that. Art today turns to the inner eye, seeking to interpret that which the outer eye sees, or even to create something entirely new independent of the objects of the world. This art is too powerful to be used simply as decoration. Some of it recaptures the numinous qualities of medieval art. Good contemporary art cannot rest content simply with showing us what Jesus may have looked like. It probes into what it must mean to be the Christ. How could God assume "the nature of a slave" and the likeness of man? How can it be that the divine manifests itself supremely under the form of a

153

suffering servant? These are questions posed eloquently in the works of such painters as Georges Rouault and many another contemporary artist.

The problem before Protestants is whether we can use such art in our worship or not. Protestants have good reason to be cautious about welcoming it. Modern liturgical art is powerful. Our worship would never be the same if we adopted it. We cannot take casually art which presents the divine. We can smash it, but we cannot ignore it. It may well be argued that there is still danger of idolatry in welcoming liturgical art into our churches. We profess to see this danger among our Catholic contemporaries, though we are not always careful to listen to their explanation of the difference between liturgical art as the object of worship and as a means in aiding their worship.

On the other hand, it can be argued that worship without liturgical art can be tempted to forget the object of its adoration also. There is danger of worship degenerating into an event in which we merely seek to receive a worshipful experience. This is a symptom of another form of idolatry, the service of self. Good liturgical art makes us aware of that which is far beyond ourselves or any material object. Its function is always to point beyond itself in order to make us aware of the presence of the God whom we worship.

The Nature of Liturgical Architecture

Whatever Protestants feel about liturgical art, there can be no escaping the use of one art form, that of architecture. Even the Quakers find architecture necessary, though they avoid the use of the other arts.

There are three basic ways of evaluating the architecture which houses common worship. These can be called technical, emotive, and liturgical.

Every building is a machine, and churches are no exceptions. Machines are judged by how efficiently they perform the function for which they are designed. In this respect the *technical* aspects of a church building are most important. They remain, however, largely the responsibility of the architect. A good architect will be able to handle such matters as heating, lighting, ventilation, and acoustics, to say nothing of structure. The architect may need to consult with specialists in these areas, but they remain primarily his concern. Though most of us do not need to be reminded how important these matters are to the operation of the church, they remain technical matters and must be entrusted to someone who has the proper technological training.

Of much greater interest to most people is the *emotive* content of the building. This is the power of the building to create an emotional response. Every building conditions our behavior to a certain extent, whether we are conscious of it or not. We respond to the totality of an interior more immediately than to special details about it. Often we hear people speak of a church as having a worshipful atmosphere. Atmosphere is another way of expressing emotive content. When people speak of a church as having a worshipful atmosphere, they are saying it has the type of emotive power which suggests worship to them.

It is very difficult to analyze the various emotive factors of a building separately, since people react to the entire interior and not to details of it. Such matters as height, the use of color, the source and intensity of lighting, and the texture of materials are important factors. Others could be added to these. It is strange, however, that there are so few constants. Excessive height does seem to create a worshipful atmosphere in the minds of most people. But how about lighting for example? Some people prefer a church "casting a dim religious light"; others demand a well-illuminated interior. The variety of reactions to these different stimuli shows how much

155

of a personal matter emotive content is, and indicates that personal associations do a great deal to determine our responses. What one man considers a worshipful atmosphere may not fit another man's definition of the same thing if their experiences have been different. Most likely, our concept of a worshipful atmosphere will be determined by the churches in which we have been accustomed to worshiping previously. Thus the emotive content of each building will vary with the individual worshiper.

In recent years there has been a great deal of interest in designing churches with careful attention to their emotive content. Much of the emphasis has been misplaced because this is not the most important feature of a church, as has so often been assumed. These matters are of primary importance in creating an atmosphere for personal devotions. The chief function of a church, however, is not to provide a setting for personal devotions, but to set the stage for common worship. Too much concentration upon creating a worshipful atmosphere has often turned church architecture into a kind of mood-setting scenery. Some contemporary churches have all the lighting gadgets and gimmicks of a well-equipped theater, and the minister or ushers try to manipulate the congregation through the use of sound and light.

The consequence has often been a tendency to forget the real nature of Christian common worship as work done together rather than as simply a matter of feeling. In common worship we do our proper service, "our bounden duty," when we perform our work of worship. With too much emphasis on worship as feeling, we are in danger of forgetting that the end of worship is God, not our own self-seeking feelings.

The *liturgical* criteria of church architecture are the best means of evaluating a church building. The basic interest here is in seeing how the building functions in common worship. Does it provide the proper tools for common worship or does it impede it? The questions which these criteria raise are primarily theological ones, and this is why they are so vitally important. Three areas of concern appear in formulating the liturgical criteria of a church.

First of all, questions have to be raised about the *design of the liturgical centers*. The liturgical centers are such objects as pulpit, altar table, baptismal font or baptistry, and other places where some specific act is performed in worship. Protestants agree that such spots have no sanctity in themselves but that what is done at them, the preaching of the Word and the Word made visible in the sacraments, are sacred acts. The design of the liturgical centers can be eloquent ways of stating the beliefs of the community which uses them in its worship. Do they conceive of Holy Communion primarily as a sacrifice or as a meal of commemoration? One form of altar may emphasize the former concept; a table may stress the later. These concepts are not mutually exclusive, but the theological predilection of the congregation may show in choosing a table or an altar.

The placement of the liturgical centers is the second concern. Indeed, one of the best ways to study the function of a church in common worship is to draw a floor plan and to indicate on it the location of the liturgical centers. Floor plans tell more about how a building is meant to operate than sketches of façades and interiors. Are the liturgical centers placed so as to enable the entire congregation to join in their common work of worship together, or do they tend to impede this? One concept of baptism may be stated by having the font set in a corner where it becomes the center of private services of dedication. Another concept, that of the child being engrafted into the church, may be emphasized when the font is placed before the congregation. Some congregations have been excited by what happens to their worship simply by moving the liturgical centers in an existing building.

157

A third component of the liturgical criteria of a building is the *location of the congregation*. Do we understand our worship as a spectacle witnessed by the congregation? This is what many Protestant and Roman Catholic churches seem to indicate. Or are the members of the congregation the actors themselves? A few recent Methodist churches gather the congregation about the altar-table as the family of God. The change in worship has been dynamic, for the people find themselves on the stage performing their worship instead of simply watching the minister. The placement of the choir is a particularly perplexing problem here, and raises questions about whether the function of the choir is to lead congregational singing or to make its own musical offering. The next few years will see many experiments, with the congregation gathered about the liturgical centers instead of being separated from them.

These three areas of liturgical criteria are the responsibility of the congregation. Unfortunately, most congregations and their building committees do not take them seriously, preferring to concentrate instead upon the emotive factors. Yet if these matters are not carefully investigated, good church architecture is impossible. The architect can do no better than the instruction he receives from the congregation. Two very serious questions have to be faced by any congregation before they are ready to build. They must give careful attention to the question, "What is the church?" and then to the query, "What does the church do when it worships?" Neither of these can be easily answered, for they are profound theological questions; yet no congregation is ready to build until it has grappled with these questions. Only then can it define the liturgical criteria which will best express its concept of worship.

The church building has other functions besides that of worship. Most of the people who see a church building never enter its doors. The majority of the buildings which we see today are seen as we move past them in our cars. This does not mean that they are meaningless to us. Any businessman knows better. There has been a great deal of interest in architecture as creating an image for a firm and this has led to some of the best—and some of the worst— of modern architecture. A church building by its very visibility is a witness for or against our faith. During the last war one chaplain found he could begin talks to soldiers, many of whom had no religious faith, by taking for granted that all at least had seen a church. For many this has been their only contact with Christianity.

The building, then, can make a real witness. Those outside the church may have little else to judge Christianity by except the exterior of its buildings. The exterior of the church has a role of proclamation; in its own way it will answer or point to the answers of questions about the church. "Is it relevant?" is a question people often ask about the church. Too often, by clothing itself in period costume, the church says it is not relevant. People often question the sincerity of the church. We must admit that many church buildings arouse their suspicions with cheap materials purporting to be what they are not and pretensions as absurd as the false-front stores of the gold-rush days. On the other hand, people want to know if the Christian faith is significant and meaningful, and again the witness of our buildings is often doubtful. Certainly architecture does not answer these questions fully, yet it may proclaim enough of the answer to invite further inquiry. Bad and irrelevant architecture discourages further interest in Christianity and hinders the mission of the church.

Christians have always considered the interior of their churches as far more important than the exteriors. This is in contrast to many other religions. The worshipers rarely got inside the Greek temples, their beauty being lavished on the exterior. But for the Christian, being in the church means participating together in its common worship. The church has always concentrated its art primarily on the interior of its buildings. This is where God's people meet to

159

renew their convenant. In a real sense each church is primarily a meetinghouse. The interior itself always speaks of what it means to be within the community of believers. Thus the interior has always had a teaching function in portraying and interpreting the life of the community. This comes about in worship but also in many other ways. Most churches today include large educational plants. Their basic function is to help those within the community to understand better the faith which makes them one. Facilities for social activities, such as dining halls, kitchens, lounges, and recreational rooms, abound in many churches. Being in the Christian community means a close union to one's fellow Christians, and knowing them is a part of this union. All these facilities are subsidiary to the sanctuary in which the church worships, yet they play an important role in teaching the meaning of the faith to those who are within or looking to joining the community of believers.

Liturgical Architecture in Protestantism

Church architecture can often be a very good index to the concepts of worship held by those who build. The buildings erected during the late medieval period are excellent examples of what had happened during the centuries preceding the Reformation. As common worship became more and more professionalized, the priests became increasingly detached from the worshipers. Gradually, the priest came to face the altar instead of the people, and the altar was pushed to the east wall at the end of the chancel furthest from the congregation. Indeed, the chancel came to be regarded as a separate building from the church proper. The chancel was for the worship of the priests; the nave, for that of the laity. The priests and those in religious orders were shut off from the laity by a screen, sometimes almost opaque. Meanwhile, the laity tried to follow the Mass at a distance, but often contented themselves with the various devotions whose symbols adorned the nave. The architectural arrangement spoke eloquently of the breakdown in the concept of the church as the whole people of God.

The Protestant Reformers inherited thousands of medieval churches designed for worship which in many ways was quite different from that which they advocated. For many years Protestants occupied medieval buildings, gradually adapting them for Protestant worship. Usually this meant making some radical changes in the arrangement of the building. A fascinating variety of experiments were conducted in creating satisfactory arrangements for Protestant worship. In some English churches the communicants actually entered the chancel at the words "draw near" in the Communion service. Frequently the table was placed in the center of the chancel running parallel to the choir stalls. In other churches the table might be moved into the nave when the sacrament was celebrated. The chief concern in all these experiments was "convenience," which might well be interpreted as "utility" or "function" in our time.

In the seventeenth century (the second century of the Reformation), Protestants first began to erect a large number of churches. For the most part they showed little inclination to copy the medieval church, with its double rectangle of chancel and nave. Indeed, most of the Protestant churches were of what may be called a central type. There were a variety of shapes for the central church type—square, Greek cross, circular, octagonal—but the common concern seemed to be that of grouping the congregation as closely as possible about the liturgical centers, particularly the pulpit. Galleries came to be almost a trademark of Protestant churches. Everything was calculated to make it possible for the congregation to follow the service with ease and to take an active part in it. Each tradition had a few distinctive characteristics in its churches or meetinghouses, the Quakers being the most radical.

John Wesley, the great Methodist leader of the eighteenth century, built several preaching houses. Their function was not that of

161

being a substitute for the parish church but of supplementing it. The Holy Communion was to be received at the parish church whenever possible, but the Methodist preaching house was to provide the possibility of preaching and other special services. Wesley had some strong opinions on the form which the preaching houses were to take. He preferred to see them built in the shape of an octagon with a high pulpit, making the preacher visible to those in the galleries and on the floor below. When Methodism became separate from the Church of England, various changes appeared in the preaching houses or chapels, such as the introduction of baptismal fonts. Communion tables had gradually appeared in most of them.

Most of us are familiar with the auditorium churches built by Protestants during the nineteenth century. The purpose of these churches was chiefly to make it possible for a large congregation to hear the preaching, which was often of a revivalistic nature. Later in the century Protestants began to build large educational plants, and frequently the auditorium and Sunday school were united in a form known as the Akron plan. The Akron plan was characterized by sloping floors with concentric rows of pews, large galleries, and sliding partitions to increase the space on certain occasions. Aesthetically most of these buildings have little to recommend them, but they do reflect the type of service of the time with its tendency to concentrate on a pulpit personality.

A rather different current in the nineteenth century was to have an even more enduring impression on Protestantism. This was Romanticism, with its great love of the past as viewed through rose-colored glasses. In England the Cambridge Movement actively promoted the revival of medieval architecture and all its accoutrements. The proponents of this revival assumed that the Middle Ages saw the highest development of Christian worship. This led them to work for the recovery of Gothic architecture, and especially for the separation of church buildings into distinct chancels and naves, a division almost completely lacking in Protestant church buildings of the eighteenth and nineteenth centuries. They also vigorously promoted the revival of medieval symbolism. Instead of designing a church with function as the primary guide, they introduced symbolism as a factor in planning the building.

It is indeed remarkable that such a return to the Middle Ages should have an appeal within Anglicanism. It is even more remarkable that Protestants of other denominations should have felt called upon to follow suit. But this is precisely what has happened. Before World War II many Protestant congregations built Gothic churches, frequently complete with the same decorations which their forefathers had destroyed. The neo-medieval church arrangement, now called the divided chancel, was adopted wholesale by Protestants, and even promoted by a board of The Methodist Church. Whether the style was Gothic, Georgian, or contemporary, the arrangement remained the same double rectangle of chancel and nave which the Reformers had found so troublesome.

In recent years the liturgical movement has led to some radical experiments in efforts to get away from the stereotyped divided chancel. One sees a renewal of the type of experimentation which followed the Reformation of the sixteenth century. The central church plan seems to be gaining favor again. New interest in the theological significance of the design of the liturgical centers is seen in an increasing use of Communion tables rather than altars, even in Roman Catholic churches. Frequently the table is placed in the center of the church, sometimes with the pulpit behind it or beside it, in an effort to obtain a more meaningful position for the liturgical centers than their aloof position in the chancel permitted. Often the congregation is located around the table and pulpit, giving dramatic emphasis to the priesthood of all believers. These experi-

163

ments take courage, and none of them can claim to be completely successful. But they are indicative of a deep and serious search to find liturgical architecture which will best help the people of God do their proper service of worship. The next few years promise to be among the most exciting in the history of Protestant liturgical architecture.

glossary

Absolution—A pronouncement of God's forgiveness and pardon. It is often written as a prayer prayed by the minister following a prayer of confession. In prayer form it is more properly called a prayer of or for pardon. See an example in the Communion ritual.

Acolyte—The unordained person, usually a boy, who assists the priest in a Roman Catholic or Anglican service. Sometimes used in The Methodist Church for the person who lights and extinguishes the candles on the Communion table, if these are used ceremonially.

Agnus Dei—A Latin phrase meaning "Lamb of God," and used to designate the hymn, "O Lamb of God that takest away the sins of the world." It is a term which also names the symbols or signs which represent Jesus as the Lamb of God.

Altar—The Communion table. Originally, any place on which sacrifices were made. In Methodist churches, the altar rail at which the people kneel for Communion or acts of prayer is often incorrectly called the altar.

Anamnesis—A Greek word usually translated "remembrance." The word also designates the part of the Holy Communion where the words of Jesus, "This do in remembrance of me," are quoted. The word means far more than mere remembering, and includes an appropriation of the facts remembered.

Anaphora—The Greek word used to designate the prayer of consecration in the Eastern Orthodox churches.

Anthem—A musical composition usually set to words from the Bible or other Christian texts. The anthem is usually sung only by the choir in a service of worship. Its attitude is generally that of praise to God.

Baptistry—The place in the church building set aside for baptisms. In Methodism this is generally at the font near or in the chancel. Any place where baptism is performed by any of the accepted modes of baptism—immersion, pouring, or sprinkling. It often is used to name the pool used for immersion in some denominations.

Basilica—A rectangular church, often flanked by aisles marked by columns. At one end of the nave, usually on the east, was an apse—a semicircular area. The term is now also used for certain distinguished Roman Catholic churches, the most famous of which is St. Peter's in the Vatican.

Benedictus—A New Testament hymn from Luke 1:68-79.

Byzantine—An adjective taken from the name of the city which has been variously called Byzantium, Constantinople, and Istanbul. The term is used to designate the church architecture of a period between the fourth and fifteenth centuries, which was characterized by domes, squares, round arches, and elaborate and colorful mosaics. The fullest use of Byzantine church architecture was developed in the Orthodox churches, where highly stylized art forms expressed the interior of the church to represent the kingdom of God.

Canticle—A nonmetrical hymn or song of praise to be said or chanted. Though the psalms are properly canticles, the term usually refers to the hymns or songs from the Bible outside the book of Psalms and many such songs of praise used by the early church which are chiefly composites of biblical passages.

Catechumen—An ancient term used to designate those who were studying the catechism and undergoing various disciplines prior to baptism which would admit them to partake of the sacrament of Holy Communion. The service of worship in the early church included the catechumens in the early part of the service (called antecommunion), and then they were dismissed before the offertory which started the Communion.

Cathedral—The word is derived from the Latin word meaning "chair." The bishop's chair in the principal church of his area in the Roman church was the seat of his administration; thus this church was called the cathedral. In Methodism there is no proper use for the term.

Chancel—The area of the church building which contains the Communion table, and often the pulpit and reading desk, the altar rail, and the choir.

Collect—A short prayer which contains an address to God, the particular attribute of God addressed, a petition in keeping with this attribute, the grace to be received by this petition, the close in the name of Jesus Christ, and the Amen. The word may come from the practice of collecting the thoughts of the Scriptures or the people by the minister into one brief prayer. See an example in the Collect for Purity at the opening of the Communion service.

Comfortable words—Scripture sentences emphasizing God's pardon and strength usually read following a prayer of confession. The English word comfort in this context draws upon a little-used meaning which signifies aid and encouragement instead of ease or softness.

Communion—A term for the sacrament of the Lord's Supper emphasizing the oneness of the church with its Lord and the fellow members. Usually called Holy Communion.

Crucifix—A cross which usually contains the figure of Jesus crucified upon it. Most Free Churches use the cross without the figure (*corpus*) to signify the death and resurrection.

Ecclesiastical directions—In an early period of church building the Communion table was toward the east. Thus in church buildings, regardless of compass directions, the chancel is east. The north is on the left of the worshiper as he faces the table, and is called the gospel side, because this was the position from which the Gospel was read in early churches. The right hand side of the worshiper is south, and is known as the epistle side, from which the Old Testament and the epistles were read. The main entrance of the church is west.

Ecumenical—From two Greek words meaning the "whole world." The term refers most frequently in Protestantism to the movement which includes all Christians and denominations in a new recognition of the oneness of the body of Christ—the church.

Epiclesis—A prayer or portion of prayer which invokes the blessing of God the Holy Spirit on the congregation and/or bread and wine.

The Eucharist—The word means "thanksgiving," and emphasizes the great thanksgiving offered to us by God through Jesus Christ. A word used increasingly throughout the churches most active in the ecumenical movement to designate Holy Communion.

Font—The fount used to contain the water for baptism by sprinkling or pouring.

Fraction—The act of breaking the bread in the Communion service. One of the four principal actions of the Eucharist.

Free Church—A term used to designate those churches which do not require a fixed ritual for their services, but which include extempore prayers and a selection of hymns and scripture readings. The term "free" does not mean without an order of worship but rather more freedom within an order.

Gloria in excelsis—The canticle used in the service of Holy Communion beginning, "Glory be to God on high."

Gloria Patri—A doxology to the Trinity beginning, "Glory be to the Father." It usually follows a psalm or other act of praise. It is generally thought that this was used as a Christian ending to the Old Testament psalm.

Gospel song—A song usually based on some New Testament idea which is an encouragement or admonition to the singers rather than directed to God.

Gradual—A musical response sung following the first scripture lesson. Since the fourth or fifth centuries it has been the musical response made while the priest moved from the epistle side to the gospel side of the chancel.

Hymn—A musical setting for praise or prayer, the words of which are usually directed to God.

Introit—A song usually from Scripture which marks the opening of the worship service. Usually the words are a call to worship or a recognition of God's call to his people.

Invitation to Christian discipleship—A section designated near the close of most Methodist orders of worship. A call to respond to the Word made known in the service. It is the invitation to offer our lives to God. The response may be in the form of an affirmation or reaffirmation of faith, decision to unite with the church, or some other commitment to live the life of obedience in the days ahead.

Koinonia—A name for the church, or the body of believers. A Greek word meaning a partnership which is more than the sum of its parts. The church as *koinonia* is more than the membership of its people; it is the membership of the body with Christ as head. Or it is the community of the church gathered in the name of Jesus Christ. "Let your bearing towards one another arise out of your life in Christ Jesus." (Phil. 2:5 NEB.)

Kyrie eleison—Greek meaning, "Lord, have mercy." This ancient response used in the churches of the East and West has been emphasized as a penitential plea to God and also as an acclamation of praise. The latter interpretation was probably the earlier, and was a supplication made in the light of the mercy of God made known in Jesus Christ.

The Last Supper—A name for Holy Communion drawn from the remembrance of the Passover meal of Jesus and his apostles prior to the Crucifixion.

Lectern—The stand or desk within the chancel on which the Bible rests and from which it is read. Where the chancel has both lectern and pulpit, the sermon is preached from the pulpit. Where there is only one stand, the term "lectern" is not used and the pulpit is used for both reading and preaching.

Lectionary—A designated plan of reading from the Bible in church and home for daily and/or weekly use. The Methodist Church has a weekly lectionary suggested for use in the churches, including three lessons for each Sunday of the year. Other denominations have lectionaries for one or two years, including a psalm and two or three scripture lessons for daily and Sunday use.

Litany—From a Greek word meaning prayer or supplication. In our present usage it is a series of prayers spoken by the minister and responded to by the congregation with brief petitions such as, "Lord, have mercy upon us."

Liturgical—A word from two Greek words meaning "the work of the people." A liturgical service, therefore, is one in which all the people gathered participate actively and responsibly in the service of worship. Nonliturgical worship is thus a service in which the congregation is present chiefly as spectator or auditor.

Liturgical colors—The colors used by churches in their altar covers or hangings. There is no one set of colors, but it is generally agreed that white is the color of celebration of the great festival seasons such as Easter and Christmas. Blue and violet are chiefly used in seasons of penitence and preparation such as Lent and Advent. Green and red are often used to designate the seasons of obedient response such as Epiphany, Pentecost, and Kingdomtide. Black or purple is used for mourning—as on Good Friday.

169

The liturgy—The name used by the Orthodox churches to designate the sacrament of Holy Communion, with its strong emphasis on Christ's resurrection.

The Lord's Supper—The name for Holy Communion which emphasizes not only the Last Supper but also the meals at which the risen Christ appeared to the believers.

Magnificat—A New Testament hymn from Luke 1:46-55.

Manual acts—The acts of the minister during the prayer of consecration in the Communion service, in which he takes the bread and cup in his hands as they are mentioned in the prayer.

Maranatha—An Aramaic term meaning, "Lord, come," which became one of the earliest prayers of the church in the language spoken by Jesus. It may be found in the New Testament (cf. Rev. 22:20) and the earliest records of the church's worship. It may be written in several ways to change the tense, and therefore may mean, "Our Lord has come," or, "Our Lord will come."

The Mass—The designation of Holy Communion of the Roman Catholic Church since the fifth century. The word probably comes from the words of dismissal, *Ite missa est*. These words involved the blessing which was pronounced as the service ended, and implied the whole sacramental service.

Maundy Thursday—Thursday of Holy Week. The word comes from the first word (*Mandatum*) of the prayer of the Roman Catholic Church for the washing of the feet, the act of Jesus following the meal recorded in John 13.

Narthex—The vestibule of a church. The section of the church building just next to the entrance into the nave or main room of the church.

Nave—The main body of the church in which the congregation is usually gathered. A word meaning ship in Latin, an early symbol of the church used today in the seal of the World Council of Churches.

Nunc Dimittis—A New Testament hymn from Luke 2:29-32.

Oblation—An offering of a sacrifice to God. A giving of one's self or symbol of one's self.

Offertory—The word is used to designate the act of dedication in worship symbolized by the giving of money. In some orders of worship (Orthodox and Roman Catholic in particular) there may be the offering of the bread and wine to be consecrated in the service. This is called the great offertory in the East. In a limited sense it is used to identify the psalm or anthem which is sung by the choir during the giving of the gifts. The latter use is found in the Roman Catholic service of Mass and to some extent in Protestant services.

Pericope—A portion of scripture read in a service of worship.

Postlude—An instrumental musical composition played as the congregation leaves the worship service.

Prelude—An instrumental musical composition played prior to the worship service as the congregation gathers.

Processional—An act, usually performed by the choir and ministers, symbolizing the gathering of the church for worship. It is most frequently accompanied by a processional hymn sung by all the people as the choir moves from the narthex to the chancel.

Psalter—The collection of the psalms used in worship.

Pulpit—The place from which the sermon is preached. It is usually raised and frequently enclosed on three sides. In many Protestant churches the pulpit is in a central position, and has become the place from which the Scriptures are read, the sermon preached, prayers led, and the service conducted.

Recessional—The act symbolizing the gathered church scattering into the world following worship. As in the processional, a hymn is usually sung by the people as the choir and ministers leave the chancel and move toward the narthex.

Responsive reading—A reading which alternates between the leader and the congregation. Usually the reading is from Psalms and other sections of the Bible. Traditionally, this reading is an act of praise following the movement of confession and assurance of pardon, though often it is considered as a scripture lesson. The wide selection of biblical passages and, in some hymnals, nonbiblical readings has given rise to many questions as to the real function of the responsive reading in Christian worship. Reading in alternate verses or sentences has been practiced for many centuries in the reading of psalms which are clearly antiphonal.

Ritual—A term used in several meanings. The ritual may designate the book which contains the words and orders of services of worship. The ritual may mean the words of the services. More broadly the term is used to designate not only the words but the order in which the whole service is presented.

Rubric—A direction to the worshiper written in the ritual or order of a worship service. The word comes from a Latin word meaning red (*rubrica*), because the early service books usually lettered these directions in that color.

Sacrament—An act or acts of worship instituted by Jesus. Protestants generally recognize two: baptism and Holy Communion. Roman Catholics recognize seven: baptism, confirmation, Holy Communion, penance, matrimony, ordination, and extreme unction. Sacraments are acts by the worshipers which use outward and visible symbols of that which God is doing for man and not what man is doing for God. The symbols and acts—poured or sprinkled or covering water, broken bread and distributed wine—are the common elements of life used by God to make his presence known.

Sacristy—A room in a church where the utensils used in the sacraments are kept and the preparation for the sacraments is made.

Sanctuary—The term given to a consecrated place. In the Temple in Jerusalem the Holy of Holies was the sanctuary. In church architecture the part of the church building within the chancel containing the Communion table or altar is usually separated from the rest of the church by a kneeling rail. The term is widely used in Protestantism to designate the whole room used by the church for worship.

Sanctus—The Latin word used to identify the ancient doxology from Isa. 6:3 which has become the basis for the Christian doxology used in most rituals of Holy Communion: "Holy, Holy, Holy, Lord God of hosts: Heaven and earth are full of thy glory! Glory be to thee, O Lord most High!" In the Methodist Holy Communion the *Sanctus* is preceded by the preface beginning, "Therefore with angels and archangels. . . ."

Sarum Rite—The form of the Mass current in the medieval diocese of Salisbury, England, and in much of the province of Canterbury.

Sermon—An address by the minister in a service of worship which is expected to be a contemporary and relevant proclamation of the Word of God. The sermon has its heritage in the prophetic tradition as well as the early church. Its place in the church's worship has varied from the primary to the almost ignored. The Protestant emphasis has insisted that the sermon is one of the chief vehicles by which God's Word is made known to those both inside and outside the church. God's Word gives validity to both the preaching and the sacraments—and the entire worship of the church.

Sursum Corda—The opening of the consecration section of the sacrament of the Lord's Supper which takes this title from the first words of the call

172

and response in Latin. "Life up your hearts." *Response:* "We lift them up unto the Lord." The services of both the Eastern and Western churches have used this form, the first two lines coming from early Christian use, and the remainder coming from the Jewish benediction over the "cup of blessing."

Te Deum—A famous canticle of the early church beginning, "We praise thee, O God; we acknowledge thee to be the Lord." More properly called by its first three words in Latin, *Te Deum laudamus,* the *Te Deum* is a nonscriptural hymn, though verses from several psalms were added later. The authorship has been attributed to Ambrose and Augustine, but it is more generally agreed that it was probably written by someone else.

Venite—The Latin name given to the ancient song of Judaism and the church beginning, "O come, let us sing unto the Lord." The form used in morning prayer in the Book of Common Prayer and in *The Methodist Hymnal* is Ps. 95:1-7; 96:9, 13.

Versicle—A brief verse said or sung by the minister and responded to by the people. It is frequently used as an indication of one movement of the worship service to another. This form characterizes some calls to the congregation (sometimes called suffrages) to join in prayer or praise, such as: *Minister:* The Lord be with you. *Answer:* And with thy Spirit. *Minister:* Let us pray.

Vestments and other robes—Vestments are ceremonial garments worn by the clergy during worship. In some Protestant churches the term is applied to a pulpit gown closely related to Martin Luther's use of his academic gown for preaching. The Geneva and John Wesley gowns are modifications of men's fashions previously current. Choir robes often follow the same tradition.

　　Stole—A long, narrow band worn about the neck and falling in the front. This is worn as a symbol of ordination and is sometimes thought to signify the yoke of Christ. Methodist ministers sometimes wear the stole with the Geneva gown; frequently the color of the stole follows the colors used in the church year.

　　Surplice—An outer garment of white worn over a robe or skirt. The surplice is sometimes used in Methodist churches by choirs. In the Roman Catholic and Anglican churches the surplice is worn by the priests over the cassock, or fitted robe.

bibliography

I. THEOLOGY OF WORSHIP

A. General:

Abba, Raymond. *Principles of Christian Worship.* New York: Oxford University Press, 1957.

von Allmen, Jean-Jacques. *Worship: Its Theology and Practice.* New York: Oxford University Press, 1965.

Casel, Odo. *The Mystery of Christian Worship.* Westminster, Md.: Newman Press, 1960.

Davis, Charles. *Liturgy and Doctrine.* New York: Sheed & Ward, paperback, 1961.

Edwall, Pehr, Hayman, Eric, and Maxwell, W. D., eds. *Ways of Worship.* New York: Harper & Row, 1951.

Nicholls, William. *Jacob's Ladder: The Meaning of Worship.* Richmond, Va.: John Knox Press, paperback, 1958.

Otto, Rudolf. *The Idea of the Holy.* New York: Oxford University Press, paperback, 1950.

Rattenbury, J. E. *Vital Elements of Public Worship.* London: Epworth Press, 1936.

Reed, Luther. *Worship.* Philadelphia: Fortress Press, 1959.

Schmemann, Alexander. *Introduction to Liturgical Theology.* San Diego, Calif.: American Orthodox, 1967.

Sperry, Willard. *Reality in Worship.* New York: The Macmillan Co., 1925.

Underhill, Evelyn. *Worship.* New York: Harper & Row Torchbook, 1957.

Verheul, Ambrosius. *Introduction to the Liturgy.* London: Burns & Oates, 1968 (RC).

White, James F. *The Worldliness of Worship.* New York: Oxford University Press, 1967.

THE CELEBRATION OF THE GOSPEL

B. Sacramental:

Arndt, Elmer J. *The Font and the Table.* Richmond, Va.: John Knox Press, paperback, 1967.

Aulén, Gustaf. *Eucharist and Sacrifice.* Philadelphia: Fortress Press, 1958.

Baillie, Donald M. *The Theology of the Sacraments.* New York: Scribner's, 1957.

Barclay, Alexander. *Protestant Doctrine of the Lord's Supper.* Glasgow: Jackson, Wylie, 1927.

Barth, Karl. *The Teaching of the Church Regarding Baptism.* London: SCM paperback, 1959.

Beasley-Murray, George R. *Baptism in the New Testament.* New York: St. Martin's Press, 1961.

Brilioth, Yngve. *Eucharistic Faith and Practice, Evangelical and Catholic.* New York: Seabury Press, 1966.

Clark, Neville. *An Approach to the Theology of the Sacraments.* London: SCM paperback, 1958.

Cullmann, Oscar. *Baptism in the New Testament.* London: SCM paperback, 1961.

Dix, Gregory. *Theology of Confirmation in Relation to Baptism.* London: Dacre Press paperback, 1953.

Eucharistic Theology Then and Now. London: S.P.C.K. paperback, 1968.

Flemington, W. F. *The New Testament Doctrine of Baptism.* New York: Seabury Press, 1948.

Forsyth, P. T. *The Church and the Sacraments.* London: Independent Press, 1955.

Kerr, Hugh Thomson. *The Christian Sacraments.* Philadelphia: Westminster Press, 1944.

Lampe, G. W. H. *The Seal of the Spirit.* 2nd ed. Naperville, Ill.: Alec R. Allenson, 1967.

O'Neill, Colman. *New Approaches to the Eucharist.* Staten Island, N. Y.: Alba House, paperback, 1967.

Powers, Joseph M. *Eucharistic Theology.* New York: Herder and Herder, 1967.

Quick, Oliver Chase. *The Christian Sacraments.* New York: Harper & Row, 1927.

Rahner, Karl. *The Church and the Sacraments.* New York: Herder and Herder, 1966.

Schillebeeckx, E. *Christ: The Sacrament of the Encounter with God.* New York: Sheed & Ward, 1963.

———. *The Eucharist.* New York: Sheed & Ward, 1968.

Stone, Darwell. *History of the Doctrine of the Holy Eucharist.* 2 vols. London: Longmans, Green & Co., 1909.

Thurian, Max. *The Eucharistic Memorial.* 2 vols. Richmond, Va.: John Knox Press, 1961.

Wotherspoon, Henry J. *Religious Values in the Sacraments.* New York: Scribner's, 1928.

II. GENERAL HISTORIES

Bishop, Edmund. *Liturgica Historica.* Oxford: Clarendon Press, 1962.

Davies, J. G. *A Select Liturgical Lexicon.* Richmond, Va.: John Knox Press.

Garrett, T. S. *Christian Worship, An Introductory Outline.* 2nd ed. New York: Oxford University Press, 1963.

Hislop, D. H. *Our Heritage in Public Worship.* New York: Scribner's, 1935.

Maxwell, W. D. *An Outline of Christian Worship.* New York: Oxford University Press, 1936.

Micklem, Nathaniel, ed. *Christian Worship: Studies in Its History and Meaning.* New York: Oxford University Press, 1936.

Palmer, Paul. *Sacraments and Worship.* London: Darton, Longman, and Todd, paperback, 1957.

Shepherd, Massey H., Jr. *At All Times and in All Places.* Rev. ed. New York: Seabury Press, 1965.

Spielmann, Richard M. *History of Christian Worship.* New York: Seabury Press, 1966.

Thompson, Bard, ed. *Liturgies of the Western Church.* Cleveland: Meridian Books, 1961.

III. SPECIFIC HISTORICAL PERIODS

A. Biblical:

Delorme, J. *et al.* *The Eucharist in the New Testament.* Baltimore: Helicon Press, 1964.

Delling, G. D. *Worship in the New Testament.* Philadelphia: Westminster Press, 1962.

Dugmore, C. W. *The Influence of the Synagogue upon the Divine Office.* London: Faith Press, 1964.

George, A. *et al.* *Baptism in the New Testament.* Baltimore: Helicon Press, 1964.

Herbert, A. S. *Worship in Ancient Israel.* Richmond, Va.: John Knox Press, paperback, 1959.

Higgins, A. J. B. *The Lord's Supper in the New Testament.* London: SCM paperback, 1950.

177

Jeremias, Joachim. *Eucharistic Words of Jesus.* New York: Scribner's, 1966.

Kraus, Hans-Joachim. *Worship in Israel.* Richmond, Va.: John Knox Press, 1966.

Moule, C. F. D. *Worship in the New Testament.* Richmond, Va.: John Knox Press, paperback, 1962.

Oesterley, W. O. E. *The Jewish Background of the Christian Liturgy.* Oxford: Clarendon Press, 1925.

Rowley, H. H. *Worship in Ancient Israel.* Philadelphia: Fortress Press, 1967.

Worden, T. *et al. Sacraments in Scripture.* London: Geoffrey Chapman, 1966.

B. Early Church:

Aland, Kurt. *Did the Early Church Baptize Infants?* Philadelphia: Westminster Press, 1963.

Dix, Gregory. *The Shape of the Liturgy.* London: Dacre Press, 1945.

———, ed. *The Treatise on the Apostolic Tradition of St. Hippolytus of Rome.* London: S.P.C.K., 1968.

Easton, B. S., ed. *The Apostolic Tradition of Hippolytus.* Hamden, Conn.: Shoestring Press, Archon Books, 1962.

Jeremias, Joachim. *Infant Baptism in the First Four Centuries.* Philadelphia: Westminster Press, 1961.

Jungmann, Joseph. *The Early Liturgy to the Time of Gregory the Great.* London: Darton, Longman, and Todd, paperback, 1963; Notre Dame, 1959.

Srawley, J. H. *The Early History of the Liturgy.* Cambridge: Cambridge University Press, 1947.

C. Eastern Churches:

Brightman, Frank. *Liturgies Eastern and Western,* Vol. I (some untranslated). Oxford: Clarendon Press, 1896.

King, Archdale A. *The Rites of Eastern Christendom.* 2 vols. Rome: Catholic Book Agency, 1947.

Liesel, Nikolaus. *Eucharistic Liturgies of the Eastern Churches.* Collegeville, Minn.: Liturgical Press, 1963.

Salaville, Severien. *Introduction to the Study of Eastern Liturgies.* London: Sands & Co., 1938.

Verghese, Paul. *The Joy of Freedom: Eastern Worship and Modern Man.* Richmond, Va.: John Knox Press, paperback, 1967.

D. Western Rites:

Batiffol, Pierre. *History of the Roman Breviary.* London: Longmans, Green & Co., 1912.

Cabrol, Fernand. *The Mass of the Western Rites*. London: Sands & Co., 1934.

Fortescue, Adrian. *Ceremonies of the Roman Rite Described*. London: Burns, Oates, and Washbourne, 1934.

Jungmann, Joseph A. *The Mass of the Roman Rite*. 2 vols. New York: Benziger Bros., 1950-52.

Porter, William S. *The Gallican Rite*. London: Mowbray, paperback, 1958.

Salmon, Pierre. *The Breviary Through the Centuries*. Collegeville, Minn.: Liturgical Press, 1962.

Swete, Henry Barclay. *Church Services and Service Books Before the Reformation*. New York: The Macmillan Co., 1930.

E. Reformation Traditions:

Barkley, John M. *The Worship of the Reformed Church*. Richmond, Va.: John Knox Press, paperback, 1967.

Brightman, Frank. *The English Rite*. 2 vols. London: Riveringtons, 1915.

Brooks, Peter. *Thomas Cranmer's Doctrine of the Eucharist*. London: Macmillan & Co., 1965.

Clarke, W. K. Lowther and Harris, Charles, eds. *Liturgy and Worship*. London: S.P.C.K., 1932.

Davies, Horton M. *Worship and Theology in England*. Vol. III (1690-1850), Vol. IV (1850-1900), Vol. V (1900-1965). Princeton: Princeton University Press, 1961-65.

———. *Worship of the English Puritans*. London: Dacre Press, 1948.

Dugmore, Clifford W. *Eucharistic Doctrine in England from Hooker to Waterland*. London: S.P.C.K., 1942.

———. *The Mass and the English Reformers*. London: Macmillan & Co., 1958.

Hageman, Howard. *Pulpit and Table*. Richmond, Va.: John Knox Press, 1962.

Luther's Works. Vols. 35-38. *Word and Sacrament*. Vol. 53. *Liturgy and Hymns*. Philadelphia: Fortress Press, 1959-.

MacLeod, Donald. *Presbyterian Worship: Its Meaning and Method*. Richmond, Va.: John Knox Press, 1965.

Maxwell, W. D. *History of Worship in the Church of Scotland*. New York: Oxford University Press, 1955.

Reed, Luther D. *The Lutheran Liturgy*. Philadelphia: Fortress Press, 1947.

Richardson, Cyril C. *Zwingli and Cranmer on the Eucharist*. Evanston, Ill.: Seabury-Western Theological Seminary, paperback, 1949.

Shepherd, Massey H., Jr. *The Oxford American Prayer Book Commentary*. New York: Oxford University Press, 1950.

Sprott, George W. and Thomas, Leishman. *Book of Common Order (1564) and Directory for Public Worship (1645)*. Edinburgh: William Blackwood and Son, 1868.

Vatja, Vilmos. *Luther on Worship*. Philadelphia: Fortress Press, 1958.

Wallace, Ronald S. *Calvin's Doctrine of the Word and Sacrament*. Edinburgh: Oliver and Boyd, 1953.

White, James F. *The Cambridge Movement*. New York: Cambridge University Press, 1962.

F. Methodism:

Baker, F. *Methodism and the Lovefeast*. London: Epworth Press, paperback, 1957.

Bishop, John. *Methodist Worship*. London: Epworth Press, 1950.

Bowmer, John C. *The Lord's Supper in Methodism, 1791-1960*. London: Epworth Press, paperback, 1961.

————. *The Sacrament of the Lord's Supper in Early Methodism*. London: Epworth Press, 1951.

Cooke, Richard J. *History of the Ritual of the Methodist Episcopal Church*. Cincinnati: Jennings & Pye, 1900.

Harmon, Nolan B. *The Rites and Ritual of Episcopal Methodism*. Nashville: Cokesbury Press, 1926.

Parris, John. *John Wesley's Doctrine of the Sacraments*. Naperville, Ill.: Alec R. Allenson, 1963.

Rattenbury, J. E. *Eucharistic Hymns of John and Charles Wesley*. London: Epworth Press, 1948.

Voigt, Edwin. *Methodist Worship in the Church Universal*. Nashville: Graded Press, 1965.

IV. LITURGICAL MOVEMENT
A. General:

Bouyer, Louis. *Life and Liturgy*. London: Sheed & Ward, paperback, 1956.

Brown, Edgar, ed. *Liturgical Reconnaissance*. Philadelphia: Fortress Press, 1968.

Clarke, Neville. *Call to Worship*. London: SCM, paperback, 1960.

Constitution on the Sacred Liturgy. Collegeville, Minn.: Liturgical Press, paperback, 1964.

Davies, J. G. *Worship and Mission*. London: SCM, paperback, 1966.

Experiment and Liturgy. Toronto: Anglican Book Center, paperback, 1969.

Hebert, A. G. *Liturgy and Society*. London: Faber & Faber, paperback, 1960.

Jasper, Ronald C. D., ed. *The Renewal of Worship*. London: Oxford University Press, 1965.

King, James W. *The Liturgy and the Laity*. Westminster, Md.: Newman Press, 1963.

Koenker, E. B. *Liturgical Renaissance in the Roman Catholic Church*. Chicago: University of Chicago Press, 1954.

————. *Worship in Word and Sacrament*. St. Louis: Concordia, paperback, 1965.

McLuhan, Marshall. *Understanding Media*. New York: Signet Books, 1966.

McManus, Frederick. *The Revival of Liturgy*. New York: Herder, 1963.

McNaspy, Clement. *Our Changing Liturgy*. New York: Hawthorn Books, 1966.

Michonneau, G. *Revolution in a City Parish*. Westminster, Md.: Newman Press, paperback, 1952.

Moss, Basil, ed., *Crisis for Baptism*. London: SCM paperback, 1965.

Paton, David, ed. *The Parish Communion Today*. London: S.P.C.K. paperback, 1962.

Perry, Michael. *Crisis for Confirmation*. London: SCM paperback, 1967.

Robinson, J. A. T. *Liturgy Coming to Life*. Philadelphia: Westminster Press, paperback, 1964.

Shands, Alfred. *The Liturgical Movement and the Local Church*. London: SCM paperback, 1965.

Shepherd, Massey H., Jr., ed. *The Eucharist and Liturgical Renewal*. New York: Oxford University Press, 1960.

————, ed. *The Reform of Liturgical Worship*. New York: Oxford University Press, 1961.

Southcott, E. W. *The Parish Comes Alive*. New York: Morehouse, paperback, 1956.

Stearn, Gerald, ed. *McLuhan: Hot and Cool*. New York: Signet Books, 1969.

Swidler, Leonard, ed. *Ecumenism, the Spirit, and Worship*. Pittsburgh: Duquesne University Press, 1967.

Taylor, Michael J. *The Protestant Liturgical Renewal*. Westminster, Md.: Newman Press, 1963.

Vagaggini, Cipriano. *The Canon of the Mass and Liturgical Reform*. Staten Island, N. Y.: Alba House, 1967.

Watkins, Keith. *Liturgies in a Time When Cities Burn*. Nashville: Abingdon Press, 1969.

Webber, George. *God's Colony in Man's World*. Nashville: Abingdon Press, Apex Book, 1960.

Winward, Stephen. *The Reformation of our Worship*. Richmond, Va.: John Knox Press, paperback, 1967.

B. New Liturgies:

Associated Parishes (Episcopal), Shepherd, Massey H., Jr., ed. *Holy Week Offices.* New York: Seabury Press, 1958.

Cope, G., Davies, J. G., and Tytler, D. A. *An Experimental Liturgy.* Richmond, Va.: John Knox Press, paperback, 1958.

Church of England Liturgical Commission. *Modern Liturgical Texts.* London: S.P.C.K., paperback, 1968.

Church of South India. *The Book of Common Worship.* New York: Oxford University Press, 1963.

Consultation on Church Union. *An Order of Worship for the Proclamation of the Word of God and the Celebration of the Lord's Supper with Commentary.* Cincinnati: Forward Movement Publications, 1968.

Episcopal Church. *Prayer Book Studies.* 17 vols., especially Vol. XVII. New York: Church Pension Fund, 1950-67.

International Committee on English in the Liturgy, Inc. *The Eucharistic Prayers of the Roman Liturgy in English Translation.* Washington: ICEL (1330 Mass. Ave. N. W.), 1968.

McNierney, Stephen. *The Underground Mass Book.* Baltimore: Helicon Press, paperback, 1968.

Presbyterian Churches. *Book of Common Worship: Provisional Services.* Philadelphia: Westminster Press, paperback, 1966.

United Church of Christ. *The Lord's Day Service.* Philadelphia: United Church Press, paperback, 1964.

V. PREACHING

Abbey, Merrill R. *Preaching to the Contemporary Mind.* Nashville: Abingdon Press, 1963.

Barth, Karl. *The Word of God and the Word of Man.* New York: Harper & Row, paperback, 1957.

Brilioth, Yngve. *A Brief History of Preaching.* Philadelphia: Fortress Press, paperback, 1965.

Davis, H. G. *Design for Preaching.* Philadelphia: Fortress Press, 1958.

Farmer, H. H. *Servant of the Word.* Philadelphia: Fortress Press, paperback, 1964.

Forsyth, P. T. *Positive Preaching and the Modern Mind.* Grand Rapids: Eerdmans, paperback, 1964.

Knox, John. *The Integrity of Preaching.* Nashville: Abingdon Press, 1957.

Ritschl, Dietrich. *A Theology of Proclamation.* Richmond, Va.: John Knox Press, paperback, 1960.

Sleeth, Ronald. *Proclaiming the Word.* Nashville: Abingdon Press, 1964.

VI. PRAYER

Baelz, Peter. *Prayer and Providence.* New York: Seabury Press, 1968.
Baillie, John. *A Diary of Private Prayer.* New York: Scribner's, 1949.
Boyd, Malcolm. *Are You Running with Me, Jesus?* New York: Avon Books, 1967.
Buttrick, G. A. *Prayer.* Nashville: Abingdon Press, Apex Book, 1942.
Head, David. *He Sent Leanness.* New York: The Macmillan Co., 1965.
James, Eric, ed. *Spirituality for Today.* London: SCM, paperback, 1968.
Oosterhus, Huub. *Your Word Is Near.* Westminster, Md.: Newman Press, 1968.
Quoist, Michel. *Prayers.* New York: Sheed & Ward, 1963.
Rhymes, Douglas. *Prayer in the Secular City.* Philadelphia: Westminster Press, paperback, 1968.
Wyon, Olive. *The School of Prayer.* New York: The Macmillan Co., 1963.

VII. THE CHURCH YEAR

Davis, J. G. *Holy Week: A Short History.* Richmond, Va.: John Knox Press, paperback, 1963.
Dunkle, William F., Jr. *Values in the Church Year for Evangelical Protestantism.* Nashville: Abingdon Press, 1959.
Gibson, George M. *The Story of the Christian Year.* Nashville: Abingdon Press, Apex Book, 1945.
Horn, Edward T. *The Christian Year.* Philadelphia: Fortress Press, 1957.
McArthur, A. A. *The Evolution of the Christian Year.* New York: Seabury Press, 1955.

VIII. OCCASIONAL OFFICES

Bowman, Leroy E. *The American Funeral.* Washington, D.C.: Public Affairs Press, 1959.
Irion, P. E. *The Funeral and the Mourners.* Nashville: Abingdon Press, 1954.
Leach, W. H. *The Cokesbury Marriage Manual.* Nashville: Abingdon Press, 1959.
Mitford, Jessica. *The American Way of Death.* New York: Fawcett Books, 1964.
Vanderbilt, Amy. *Everyday Etiquette.* Garden City, N. Y.: Hanover House, 1956.

IX. THE ARTS

A. Architecture:

Atkinson, C. Harry. *How to Get Your Church Built.* Garden City, N. Y.: Doubleday & Co., 1964.

Bruggink, Donald J. and Droppers, Carl H. *Christ and Architecture.* Grand Rapids: Eerdmans, 1965.

Cope, Gilbert, ed. *Making the Building Serve the Liturgy.* London: Mowbray, 1962.

Debuyst, Frederic. *Modern Architecture and Christian Celebration.* Richmond: John Knox Press, paperback, 1968.

Dolbey, George. *The Architectural Expression of Methodism: The First Hundred Years.* London: Epworth Press, 1964.

Hammond, Peter. *Liturgy and Architecture.* New York: Columbia University Press, 1961.

————. *Towards a Church Architecture.* London: Architectural Press, 1962.

Frey, Edward S. *This Before Architecture.* Valley Forge, Pa.: Foundation Books, 1963.

Lockett, William, ed. *The Modern Architectural Setting of the Liturgy.* London: S.P.C.K., 1964.

Maguire, Robert and Murray, Keith. *Modern Churches of the World.* New York: E. P. Dutton, paperback, 1965.

White, James F. *Protestant Worship and Church Architecture.* New York: Oxford University Press, 1964.

B. Visual Arts:

Cope, Gilbert, ed. *Christianity and the Visual Arts: Studies in the Art and Architecture of the Church.* London: Faith Press, 1964.

Dixon, John. *Nature and Grace in Art.* Chapel Hill: University of North Carolina Press, 1964.

Ferguson, George. *Signs and Symbols in Christian Art.* New York: Oxford University Press, 1959.

Getlein, Frank and Dorothy. *Christianity in Modern Art.* Milwaukee: Bruce, 1961.

Glendining, Frank. *The Church and the Arts.* London: SCM, paperback, 1960.

Henze, Anton and Filthaut, Theodor. *Contemporary Church Art.* New York: Sheed & Ward, 1956.

McClinton, Katharine M. *The Changing Church: Its Architecture, Art and Decoration.* New York: Morehouse-Gorham, 1957.

C. Music:

Crisis in Church Music? Washington: Liturgical Conference, 1967.

Douglas, Winfred. *Church Music in History and Practice.* New York: Scribner's, 1962.

Lovelace, Austin and Rice, William. *Music and Worship in the Church.* Nashville: Abingdon Press, 1960.

A Prelude to the Purchase of a Church Organ. Philadelphia: Fortress Press, paperback, 1964.

Routley, Erik. *Church Music and Theology.* Philadelphia: Fortress Press, 1960.

D. Dance:

Taylor, Margaret Fisk. *A Time to Dance.* Philadelphia: United Church Press, paperback, 1967.

X. PERIODICALS

Christian Art. Monthly. 1801 West Greenleaf Avenue, Chicago, Illinois.

Churchbuildings. 3/yr. John Catt Ltd., High St., Billericay, Essex England.

Liturgical Arts. RC quarterly. 521 Fifth Avenue, N. Y. C. 10017

Liturgy. RC Quarterly. The Rev. J. D. Crichton, The Presbytery, Priest Lane, Pershore, Worcestershire, England.

Liturgy. RC 10/yr. 1330 Massachusetts Ave., N. W., Washington, D.C.

Living Worship. 10/yr. Liturgical Conference, 1330 Massachusetts Ave., N. W., Washington, D. C.

Music Ministry. Methodist music monthly. 201 Eighth Avenue South, Nashville, Tenn.

Parish and People. Anglican renewal 3/yr. St. Stephen's Lodge, Hankey Place, London, S. E. 1.

Response. Lutheran art and music quarterly. 2477 Como Avenue, St. Paul, Minn.

Studia Liturgica. International ecumenical quarterly. Postbus 2, Nieuwendam, Holland.

Work/Worship. (formerly *Versicle*). Methodist quarterly, The Rev. Thorwald Torgersen, Park Avenue, Flanders, New Jersey.

Worship. RC. 10/yr. St. John's Abbey, Collegeville, Minnesota.

Yearbook of Liturgical Studies. Collegeville, Minnesota: Liturgical Press, 1960 (annual Bibliography).

index